Float Tube Fly Fishing

Deke Meyer

Frank Amato
PORTLAND

Dedicated to:
Dietrich E.
Catherine R.
Barbara L.
And in fond memory of
Ruby Begonia, faithful mutt
and fishing companion

© **1989 Deke Meyer**
Frank Amato Publications, Inc.
PO Box 82112 • Portland, Oregon 97282
(503) 653-8108
Book Design: Joyce Herbst • Typesetting: John F. Michael
Cover Photo: Andy Anderson • Illustrations: Esther Appel
ISBN: 0-936608-71-4
Printed In U.S.A.
10 9 8 7 6 5 4 3

Deke Meyer is a full time freelancer from Monmouth, Oregon, where he lives with his wife Barbara, who has her own float tube, fly rod and reel, and vest. He sold his first article in 1978 and went full time in 1982. His articles have been featured in most of the major fly fishing and outdoor magazines.

He has a B.A. in Education from Western Oregon State College, served in the U.S. Army from 1966 to 1968, worked as an Experimental Biologist Aide I on the Deschutes River for the Oregon Department of Fish and Wildlife, and is a member of the Outdoor Writers Association of America.

Besides magazine articles, he is currently working on his next book for Frank Amato Publications, *Advanced Fly Rod Steelhead.*

If you have any comments or would like to write to the author, he can be reached through the publisher at the following address: Deke Meyer, c/o Frank Amato Publications, P.O. Box 82112, Portland, Oregon 97282.

Contents

ONE

FLOAT TUBE FREEDOM

Float tubes have come a long ways since the garage genesis belly boat made from a patched inner tube draped with a homemade canvas seat. Today's cadillac float tubes are more trustworthy and more effective fishing craft. Modern float tubes incorporate a truck tire tube covered with tough non-rotting nylon, with comfortable seats, backrests, pockets, and carrying systems. When coupled with stockingfoot waders and efficient fins, float tubing is not only easy, but a great way to catch more fish.

Float tubes offer the fisherman a more intimate fishing experience because the angler is suspended in the water, supported by what guide Ted Calvert calls a floating easy chair. The immediacy to both the water and the fish is particularly captivating, especially when fighting a hooked fish. Floating at water level brings the fight closer to the angler and any leverage advantage is reduced because the fisherman is floating, too. The size and power of the fish is, in effect, magnified.

One of these new float tubes will greatly expand your fishing horizons. Not only are farm ponds and high mountain lakes prime for float tubing, but backwater arms of reservoirs (often a choice feeding area for fish) and selected quiet streams as well. Since new streams aren't being created it makes sense to be more creative in using other available waters, and a float tube is a great way to do it.

Quietly finning along will get you closer to more stillwater fish and more bigger ones, too, because you are a silent stalker. There are no built-in noisemakers in a float tube — no resonating aluminum hull, no clanking of metal or rubbing of wood. Because you're in a silently sliding water craft, gliding along with a minimum of effort, you will also be delighted to observe undisturbed water-loving birds and animals.

WHAT TO LOOK FOR IN A FLOAT TUBE

There are many good models of float tubes on the market, ranging from economy to deluxe, with the price reflecting the quality. In a dry climate a canvas belly boat might be acceptable, but heavy duty nylon is better because it dries rapidly and won't rot or deteriorate nearly as quickly as canvas, besides being a little lighter and more tear and puncture resistant.

Modern float tubes are designed as a wedge-shape, putting more floatation support at the rear of the float tube, where the weight of the tuber is, so the fisherman sits on an even keel. The nicer float tubes have carrying handles, extra pockets, a quick-release seat buckle, and velcro tabs to secure your rod while you change flies or to a spare spool. Most float tubes include a casting apron which keeps loose fly line in your lap so the line won't get wrapped around your fins. One of the most important additions is a secondary air chamber that serves as both a backrest and a safety factor.

7

Float Tube Fly Fishing

The chances of puncturing a float tube in the course of a normal fishing day are slim. A float tube truck tire inner tube holds a large volume of air under very low pressure, less than 4 pounds per square inch. And besides, the tube and the secondary air chamber are housed in a tough nylon cover.

The standard float tube uses a 20-inch inner tube, larger models use a 22-inch tube, and ultralights use a 16-inch

---

Float Tube

The wedge design of the modern float tube puts more floatation at the rear of the tube, to support most of the weight of the float tuber.

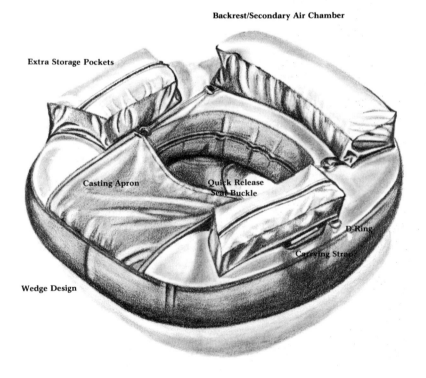

Backrest/Secondary Air Chamber

Extra Storage Pockets

Casting Apron

Quick Release Seat Buckle

D-Ring

Carrying Strap

Wedge Design

---

tube. The standard tube is sufficient to support up to 350 pounds. The larger model is designed for bigger persons or for the fisherman who wants more storage compartments or more floatation for fishing large impoundments. The main drawback to the ultralight tube and to many of the inexpensive float tubes is that they lack the safety margin of a secondary air chamber, the backrest.

There is a high degree of competition between float tube manufacturers, resulting in quality products that are competitively priced. There is a direct corollary between money spent and quality received. One of the areas to inspect is the caliber of workmanship in the stitching of the seams. The less expensive models are often not sewn well, have only single stitched seams, and have cheap zippers. If you're uncertain about a specific model of float tube or if you're wondering whether you want to try float tubing at all, one option is to investigate a rental tube. Many shops will apply the rental fee towards purchase of a float tube.

Some float tubes come with the inner tube included and some do not, requiring the customer to buy a tube at a tire shop. Another factor affecting the final price is whether the backrest/secondary air chamber includes a tube. Again, some do and some don't.

The only accessory gear absolutely necessary for float tubing is either a pair of foot paddles or swim fins. Foot paddles power the tuber in a forward direction, which is fine for casting to rising fish or working a small patch of cover. They are easier to walk in than swim fins.

But swim fins are much more efficient for moving through the water because fins power the tuber on both the forward and backward strokes, not just the forward stroke of the foot paddles. Swim fins are more difficult to walk in but are better for working a wet fly, for trolling while moving from one spot to another, and for applying reverse power for setting the hook. And with fins, once the angler is in position, by just turning the tube around the tuber can cast to rising fish or work a popper through the lily pads.

Some shops offer a package deal on both the float tube,

fins, and inner tube if not included with the float tube. A complete outfit is often your best deal. Although you can use chest waders, stockingfoot waders are the ticket for float tubing. Neoprene waders are ideal unless you fish in warm water or don't get cold easily.

The price of one of the better float tubes, a set of fins, and a pair of neoprene waders is still less than half what a small boat would cost, without considering a motor and gas tank, the trailer, oars, life jackets, licensing, and maintenance items like mixing the gas and oil, tuneups, greasing the trailer bearings and repairing flat tires.

One of the biggest advantages of float tubing is portability. A deflated float tube takes up very little room and even when fully inflated, a float tube is indeed small when compared to a boat. A compact portable air compressor that plugs into the dashboard cigarette lighter lets the angler inflate the tube at the lake, so the float tube can be transported deflated.

Float tubes offer a high degree of accessibility, too. A float tuber only needs a few square feet of open area at the water's edge to launch. A float fisherman isn't restricted to boat launches. The small fishy-looking brushy lakes that lack boat launches, the quiet structure-riddled coves of large lakes, and pastoral farm ponds are all but a few fin strokes away.

There are countless fishing spots all across the country where fish never see a fly because neither wading nor boating fishermen can get to them — but a float tuber can.

USING YOUR FLOAT TUBE

Getting in and out of your float tube might seem tricky the first time, but soon becomes as automatic as jointing up a fly rod. For the first launch, pick an area with firm footing that gradually slopes down into the lake. Set your tube with the seat unbuckled at the water's edge, facing shoreward because with swim fins it's easier to walk backwards the few steps you'll need. Set your strung-up fly rod next to the float tube where you can reach it, but not so close that you might step on it.

After donning waders, vest, and fins, first put one foot through the float tube seat, and then the other, facing the shore, not the water. If you feel yourself falling, simply sit down, regroup, and start over. No need to get in a hurry. The awkwardness will soon disappear.

Today's modern float tube incorporates a truck tire tube covered with tough non-rotting nylon, with a comfortable seat, a backrest that doubles as a secondary air chamber for safety, and includes a casting apron, pockets, and carrying systems. Photo by Randy Gunn

Float Tube Fly Fishing

After both feet are in the tube, connect the seat buckle, pick up your fly rod, pull the tube up to waist level, and back into the lake. Take your time and slowly shuffle into the water. If you feel yourself overbalancing, simply bend your knees and sit down. Once you are knee-high in the water, you can sit in the tube and begin finning out into the lake.

Propelling yourself with fins is simple because the motion is much like walking, only underwater. Unless you are trying to cover a lot of water, it takes little effort to propel your tube and is actually quite relaxing in itself. Not only is float tubing an enjoyable way to fish it is also soothing to be comfortably suspended in water.

Float tubing has a whole different feel to it. A hooked fish seems wilder when it jumps at eye level right in front of you while you fight the fish right up to the tube, practically in your lap.

Float tubing is not only fun but you can fish varied waters. One week in late June I tubed two totally different

A float tuber enjoys the closeness of the battle; being suspended in the fish's home and fighting the fish up to your lap gives the fisherman a tremendous feeling of immediate contact with the fish. Photo by Randy Gunn

types of water: on a pastoral country pond and on one of the backwater arms of Wickiup Reservoir in central Oregon.

The pond I fished is rich in aquatic life (especially midges), has stable banks, lots of vegetative cover, and maintains vigorous populations of bass and bluegill. There are bass of good size – I know, because on a previous trip one of my fly-hooked bluegill was inhaled by a bass in the 4-pound class. I landed the 'gill but the bass turned his prey loose and escaped.

But on this float tube foray my intention was to tangle with some of the larger bluegill, from 6 to 8 inches, with some going to 9-inches. It was a real treat to be quietly finning along, hooking and fighting broad-sided bluegill. The fishing was especially pleasant because I used a three-weight rod and floating line, matched to the fish. I just love to watch the rod tip dance in front of my eyes while comfortably sitting in my floating onion ring.

The trip to Wickiup was totally different. With normal precipitation, Wickiup Reservoir has over 4500 surface acres and more than 25 miles of crooked shoreline, with many little coves that are prime float tubing territory. Wickiup hosts healthy populations of both browns and rainbows, with some getting into poundage in the teens, which is more than adequate gist for a float tuber's fishing fantasies.

My fishing partner strung up a 10-foot graphite rod with a 7-weight High-Speed Hi-D full sinking line and a No. 6 Olive Matuka. I rigged my 9-foot graphite with a 7-weight floating line and a No. 10 dark brown weighted Soft Hackle nymph.

We had only been fishing for a half hour or so when I let out an excited yell as a nice brownie hit my fly on the run. The trout then leaped just off the round bow of my float tube. I can still see his arced classic spotted brown butterscotch body; his midair jump frozen in time. My partner got into some nice fish, too, doing battle farther out where his super-fast sinking line was ideal for probing the depths of the old river channel.

13

RELATED FLY FISHING GEAR

The proper fly line and matched rod and reel setup will correlate with several factors, like the size of the fish, weight and bulk of the flies used, weather conditions like wind, and to some extent, the size of the lake. Float tube fly fishing is the same as any other fly fishing in that the fly line is the crucial cornerstone of the system. The fly rodder must determine which fly line weight is appropriate for the chosen lake. Generally, most trout lakes are well fished with 6 or 7-weight lines, but smaller lakes and farm pond bluegill are matched to 3, 4, or 5-weight rigs. Big water, big flies, lunker fish, or wind can demand an 8-weight outfit, as does tossing bass poppers.

Whether you're tantalizing a brawny bass with a seductive surface popper or courting a deep bodied rainbow hanging just off the lake bottom, you not only need the proper line matched to the appropriate rod, you must be able to put your fly at the proper depth. At times you have to be something of a piscatorial soothsayer to determine where the fish will be feeding and on what. Lake fish are usually susceptible to a variety of different flies at any given time, but the location of the fish's preferred strata in the water column is of primary importance.

Water temperature, degree of cover, and availability of food all determine where fish will be in the lake structure. To be successful the lake fly rodder needs fly lines that present the fly at all depths.

Generally, the most important lines are a floater, a sinktip, and a full fast sinking line. A weight forward floating line will shoot a little farther, but a double taper can be reversed, effectively doubling its useful life. A bass bug taper is specifically designed for working a popper for bass, an excellent float tubing combination.

The sinktip and the full sinking line should be medium fast, like Scientific Anglers Wet Cel II or Hi-D, or Cortland's Type II or Type III.

Other valuable stillwater lines are the slow sinkers, like

A float tube functions much like an aquatic zoom lens, bringing the fisherman into close focus with the aqueous world of the fish, bustling nymphs, and the fascinating lacery of underwater plants. Photo by Randy Gunn

the Wet Cel I or Type I lines. The Intermediate is a dandy for working over the tops of weedbeds with the fly line just under the surface, preventing any surface disturbance which alarms trout. The High-Speed Hi-D or Type IV or even the Deep Water Express are designed for fishing very deep water.

Shooting head systems offer the advantages of painless distance casting and are easily interchanged. In many instances, covering the maximum amount of water will result in catching more fish.

Sinktip lines, with their sinking and floating sections, get the fly down but still give the angler more control than a full sinking line. The visibility of the floating part acts as a giant strike indicator.

Float Tube Fly Fishing

Sinktip lines add another valuable tool to the fly fisherman's arsenal because they are ideal for fishing ledges, dropoffs, and the deepwater edges of weedbeds. A sinktip line gives a buoyant but sunken fly an irresistible underwater action. For example, a marabou muddler attached to 3 feet of leader on the end of a sinktip would tend to sink when retrieved. But if the retrieve is stopped briefly, the pause allows the fly to drift slowly upward, only to dive downward when the retrieve is resumed. This up-and-down motion is deadly on bass and trout.

The Correct Fly Line

Choosing the correct fly line to use is very important. In illustration A, a dry line is being used and the angler is stripping in a wet fly that is slowly rising to the surface. If you want your fly to stay deeper (generally where most of the fish are) then you should use a sink tip or sinking line as shown in illustration B.

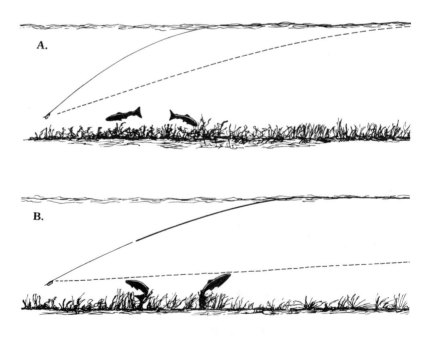

A.

B.

Once armed with spare spools with lines or shooting heads to cover any eventuality, the float tuber then needs a varied selection of flies. A lake in fine fettle can support an incredible array of aquatic insects, assorted dependent organisms like leeches and frogs, crustaceans like crawfish, and various small prey fish.

Events that radically alter feeding patterns can change from day to day. For example, a lake can host a specific hatch, like a midge or damselfly emergence, or it can be the scene of a flying ant migration.

Stillwaters vary tremendously so a floating fly fisherman needs a mixture of flies to cover all the possibilities. One approach is to contact the fly shop closest to the target lake for information on predominant hatches and productive patterns. Once at the lake a small aquarium net can be used to sample insects. Besides talking to other fishermen, another gambit is to check the stomach contents of any fish harvested from the lake.

If the fish are feeding on top, dry fly fishing can be exciting, but that only happens about 10% of the time. Most of the season you'll be probing trout and bass water with a sunken fly. One of the most crucial aspects of subsurface fishing is presenting the fly at the feeding depth of the fish.

Once at the suitable depth, the fly must behave properly; experimentation in retrieve is just as important as fly pattern. The hand-twist, strip and pause, and a vigorous stripping retrieve are all effective at times. A change in retrieve will often turn on fish that were ignoring previous casts. In the same vein, the bewitching topwater variations that the successful bass fisherman works on a popper can approach art.

Fly fishermen are becoming more and more versatile. Expanded fly line and graphite rod technologies have ushered us into the age of the spare spool. Not only is there a vast panorama of high-tech floating and sinking lines to use, but now that we have highly portable and efficient float tubes to fish from, our fishing horizons are extended even further.

TWO

READING A TROUT LAKE

The lake fly fisherman must be an angling detective, sleuthing the clues that tell where the trout are feeding and on what. A simplified version of the basic food chain of a trout lake could be described as: aquatic vegetation, aquatic insects, small fish (both baitfish and baby trout) and finally, prime gamefish like trout.

The holding attractants of vegetative insect life and prey fish cause the larger carnivorous trout to zero in on specific areas of lakes and reservoirs. While on the hunt these older fish remain wary; they are leaving the security and protection of deeper water.

The shallower regions of a lake are the most productive for both trout and fly fishermen. The highest percentage of insect life, small fish, and adult trout inhabit the upper water levels mainly because sunlight is the primary energy force that activates the food chain. Underwater plants provide a rich oxygen source for invertebrates and fish and are the food source for grazing nymphs. Aquatic vegetation

18

provides cover for rapacious dragonfly and damselfly nymphs, as well as water boatmen, diving beetles, and backswimmers. Small fish navigate the greenery, both for camouflage safety and to hunt food. Large trout search out anything that moves.

The shallow shore area that extends out to the limit of rooted aquatic plants is known as the littoral zone. The littoral zone is usually the richest area in a lake and should be thoroughly explored with the searching fly, especially during the low light conditions of early morning and late evening when insect and trout activity is at its height. Other littoral areas to probe are islands and submerged shoals or gravel tracts that support weedbeds.

One way to approach stillwater fishing is by mentally dividing the lake into quadrants. The most important quadrant is the rich littoral zone, best exploited with a full floating line, an Intermediate, or an Intermediate sinktip, for dry fly fishing or easing a nymph along just over the ceiling of a sunken weedbed.

The second quadrant is the sunken sublittoral zone out away from shore. This includes raised areas that support weedbeds, like sunken islands or aquatic growth around submerged springs. Sinktip or medium fast full sinking lines are good tools for twitching a nymph or leech imitation past the aquatic greenery.

The third quadrant is an incoming or outgoing stream, a prime feeding spot for trout. The current activates nymphs and small fish, making it a good kitchen for bigger fish. The amount of water flow and gradient will determine whether a floating or sinking line should be used.

The fourth quadrant is a deep water fishery. Jumbo trout seek out food, but still require cover. Log tangles, rock escarpments that ledge off into deeper water, or any underwater feature that offers ambush concealment will appeal to hefty trout. Constant temperature deepwater springs are choice spots for big trout during extremes of cold or hot weather. A sinktip or full sinking line is the ticket for whisking a streamer past these cannibal lairs.

The majority of the time stillwater trout are opportunist

Areas Where Fish Are Most Often Found

A lake with inlet and outlet and some possible types of structure where fish will be found either feeding or resting.

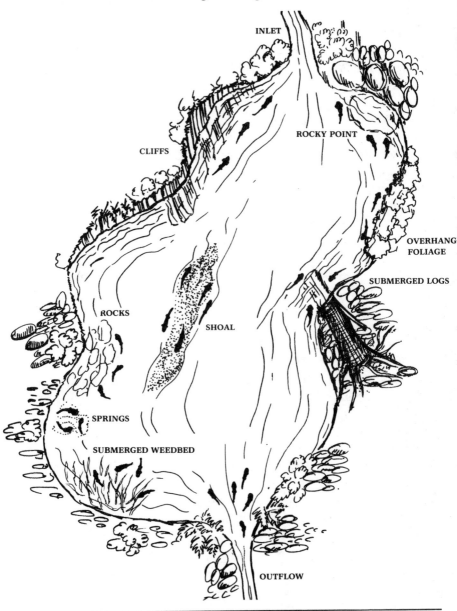

INLET

ROCKY POINT

CLIFFS

OVERHANG
FOLIAGE

SUBMERGED LOGS

ROCKS

SHOAL

SPRINGS

SUBMERGED WEEDBED

OUTFLOW

feeders, pouncing on any available food items in the aquatic larder. A hatch of midges, mayflies, damselflies, or other insects will trigger specific selective feeding activity, but overall, concentrated feeding fills only a small part of the trout's daily and yearly diet. Trout and fly fishermen welcome a hatch, but many times an overabundance of insects will result in temporarily overfed trout and blanked fishermen. Midges, mayflies, or flying ants can literally cover a lake. Unlike a stream where the insects are carried away on the current, windrows of bugs can blanket a lake, eliminating a fisherman's chances of hooking a fish.

Hatches in only part of the lake are much more workable and are not uncommon. The flat surface of a lake disguises the fact that there are little mini-ecosystems spread throughout a lake. These little communities differ because of the composition of the soil, the presence of springs and altered temperatures and alkalinity, and the gradient of the shore.

The investigative fisherman explores the shoreline and associated littoral region, ferreting out any clues about trout prey. Look in the backwash eddies for shucks that might indicate a recent midge, mayfly, or even caddis hatch. Trapped aquatic and terrestrial bugs give an indication of what is available to the trout. Spider webs and shoreside brush are well worth examining for insects. Wading the shallows and picking up patches of aquatic greenery can lend valuable clues about the size, types, and coloration of various underwater critters that trout prey on. Swishing a small aquarium net or mesh screen through the shoreline shallows works, too.

Part of being an angling sleuth is chatting with fellow fishermen about their success on the lake. What didn't work is almost as important as what did work because it narrows the possibilities a bit. A logbook can be a handy reference for approximating the time periods for major hatches.

Being a fly fishing Perry Mason and solving the mysteries of a lake is a challenge, but once you determine the nature of the food items available to the trout, the same basic rules apply to all trout fishing. These are matching the size and color of the prey, and proper presentation, which includes varying the retrieve for sunken flies and working the correct water depth with the appropriate fly line. The lake fly fisherman can easily justify carrying hundreds of flies because of the tremendous variety of organisms present in a healthy trout lake. In their fine book, *Lake Fishing With A Fly*, 1984, Frank Amato Publications, Ron Cordes and Randall Kaufmann list eleven distinct food groups available to trout in a lake's ecosystem. A good attitude to develop is to view the lake as a trout's kitchen, bearing in mind that trout will prey on anything that moves that will fit into their mouths.

The most productive fishing time during a hatch of aquatic insects or a fall of ants or mayfly spinners is at the beginning, just as the fish begin to gorge themselves. Sifting the aquatic growths is one approach to detecting an imminent hatch, but more often than not the fly fisherman will already be out on the lake when the hatch begins. Suddenly midges will be buzzing on the surface amid bulging trout, or mayflies will pop their sails, hoping to catch the wind before the trout get them.

Midges are a year round staple in the stillwater trout's diet, but the most important phase of the midge hatch for the fly fisherman is the hatching pupa. It hangs just below the surface, attempting to break through the meniscus into adulthood. An aquarium net is handy for examining the midge pupa for size and color. A good way to rig for a midge hatch is with one or two midge pupa imitations tied on a leader greased to within 6 inches of the fly, with a strike indicator for the often subtle strike. Trout tend to cruise and inhale midge pupae, expending the minimum effort to conserve energy. The presentation is dead still on a floating line, casting the flies into the cruising lane of the midging trout. A very subtle twitch can be transmitted to the flies to induce the trout to pick your offering. A super-slow hand-twist retrieve will allow you to cover more ground, but bear in mind that midge pupa don't move much once they are locked into the surface film. Your hand-twist approach would simulate pupa ascending to the surface.

Vegetative areas are a good place to hand-twist a Callibaetis mayfly nymph imitation with a floating or Intermediate or Intermediate sinktip line. The hand-twist retrieve can be interspersed with short pulls because the Callibaetis is a swimming-type mayfly and very active underwater, its dartings often resembling a small fish. Trout lakes will commonly have several broods of Callibaetis every season, so the nymphs are always present, browsing in and out of the aquatic greenery.

When the fly fisherman learns how to "read" specific stillwater clues, unravelling the mysteries of a lake can be both intriguing and rewarding. Photo by Randy Gunn

During a Callibaetis hatch an emergent pattern is often the best, either twitched in the surface film or slowly raised to the surface like the hatching insect. If the fish switch to the dun, pot shooting the rise can be fun. The cast is made to the next spot the fish is anticipated to rise. A tweak imparted to the dry will often attract a strike. The most consistent fishing occurs when the female spinners return en masse to lay their eggs. The trout will gorge on spinners unable to fly from the water's surface.

I remember one September evening on Lewis Lake in Yellowstone Park. Lewis is somewhat unique because its brown trout stocked in 1890 are pure Loch Levens originally from Scotland. The late afternoon sun slanted low over the western mountains and the light breeze was abating. The calming warm air triggered a dense Callibaetis spinner fall. The lake's smooth countertop was peppered with speckled-wing spinners, their little semaphore wings making a grand parade field.

The littoral zone extends from the edge of the shore to the point where rooted aquatic weeds and other vegetation stop. Obviously, shallow lakes have much larger littoral zones and thus are often more food rich.

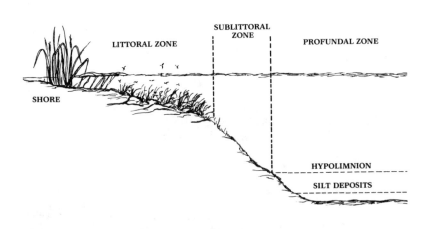

SUBLITTORAL ZONE

LITTORAL ZONE

PROFUNDAL ZONE

SHORE

HYPOLIMNION

SILT DEPOSITS

Trout began feeding in diligent rises like rain on a pond. I had strung up a heavy rod with a weight forward floating line because I wanted to make distance casts and had anticipated using a streamer for the wary browns.

As I finned into position I noticed one particular fish because of two factors: a prodigious dorsal fin that looked like a catamaran sail and secondly, the fish's eccentric habit of taking a spinner, porpoising, and then taking a second spinner before going down. It's always a little unnerving to be within casting range of a feeding bruiser trout but not know where he'll rise next.

Fortunately, my first few casts didn't line him and he kept feeding. Twice he came up very near my fly but didn't take it. All around me enthusiastic trout were noisily sucking in spinners as riseforms pockmarked the lake.

My next cast laid the fly about a foot from the big brown's first rise in a new series. He porpoised, cleaving the laketop with a dorsal fin the size of the tailfin on a '57 Chevy, then gleaned my spinner from the surface.

I raised the rod with held breath – the fish steamed out like an angry torpedo, changing direction so fast the fly line whooshed through the water, leaving a tiny roostertail of water in its wake. The fly rod bent deeply, then the tippet parted like torn wet newspaper. I felt deflated; I had forgotten to change the drag setting on the reel for the lighter tippet after steelheading the previous week.

Another prevalent lake hatch is the predacious damselfly. Although the damsels don't hatch until summer, trout feed on the nymphs from spring up until they crawl out on lakeside vegetation and hatch. Damsels are slim tan, olive, or bright green critters with a set of paddle-like tails that are also their lungs. Their sculling swimming motions are difficult to duplicate but an irregular hand-twist retrieve will often fool fish into striking.

Dragonflies are another prime entree in the lake cafeteria, especially in their robust nymphal form. Imitations are fished in an erratic manner, miming the spurts of speed the dragonfly nymph attains by expelling water from its posterior. Occasionally, trout will feed on adult damselflies and dragonflies, but not as consistently as on the nymphs.

A lake can be much more difficult to read than a stream because most of the time trout are feeding underwater, out of sight of the fisherman. In many respects a lake is like an aquatic jungle where predators become the prey of another captor, whether it's a dragonfly capturing a midge pupa, a fish eating a dragonfly, or an osprey seizing a trout in its talons.

An individual lake is like any particular trout stream. The physical and chemical makeup of each lake makes is unique and presents its own fly fishing problems. When the fly fisherman learns how to read specific stillwater clues and maps out a quadrant plan of attack, unraveling the moody mysteries of a lake can be intriguing and rewarding in its own right.

In many respects a lake is like an aquatic jungle where predators become the prey of another captor, whether it's a dragonfly capturing a midge pupa, a fish eating a dragonfly, or an osprey seizing a trout in its talons. Photo by Randy Hansen

THREE

BIG TROUT

Because of a need for greater caloric intake when trout reach 15 inches, their diet shifts from the occasional insect to more carniverous fare like smaller fish, leeches, frogs, and crayfish. An older trout becomes a more efficient hunter, hoarding its energy, feeding in concentrated bursts. Jumbo trout feed during dense hatches of aquatic insects, but a patriarchal fish can't afford to wander aimlessly in search of tidbits; the organic fuel collected wouldn't balance out the energy used to power its bigger body.

Large trout don't change their feeding habits after reading the morning paper. Theirs is an immediate world of predator and prey, a continually shifting ellipse centered on the two poles of existence: the need for food and the need for cover. With little regard for concealment, young fish are constantly on the prowl, dining randomly on insects and even smaller fish. Conversely, burly trout seek out the most protected cover, a function of instinctual wariness that allows them to grow to be the biggest trout. Mammoth trout covet hunting grounds that provide a degree of protection while still providing ambush-feeding opportunities. For big fish, cover and protection equals deep water or at least deeper water. But deep water is not rich in the aquatic insect life that supports prey like pint-sized fish, so jumbo trout must move into shallower water to feed.

MIGRATION ROUTES

Old trout will often follow particular migration routes from deeper water to favorite feeding areas. One type of underwater highway that offers cover to migrating trout is a log snag or fallen tree that abuts deeper water. Beefy trout browse the sunken timber for dragonfly nymphs and leeches that rest on the downed limbs, but their main prey is the peewee fish that seek refuge in the watery branches.

Most fly fishermen pass up these snags or merely pluck at the edges with a few timid casts. The seeker of husky fish can't be intimidated by an army of underwater arms waiting to snare the fly. Using a weedless fly puts the caster into water that may yield a real lunker. Tying dragonfly nymph, leech, and juvenile fish imitations on keel hooks or with a Dave Whitlock mono-loop weed guard or upside down bonefish-style opens up snag alley to the probing fly.

Ledges and dropoffs are another prime migration route for big fish moving from deep water to shallow hunting grounds. Bulky trout glide up out of the depths, lurking at the edge of the deep water, craving cover and security, but caving in to hunger and the need to feed. Underwater rock ledges harbor crayfish, a high-protein trout meal. Ledges with aquatic vegetation are favorite hunting grounds for carniverous trout because small fish hunt for food among the greenery.

Like the most grizzled of trout, crayfish are most active

in low light conditions. Crayfish start foraging in the evening, continue on through the night, and retire to rock crevices only when dawn fades with the full light of day. Unless startled, crayfish crawl along the bottom. When alarmed, crayfish swim backwards, propelled by their abdominal muscle tissue and flippers.

When a friend of mine is fishing for oversize trout he uses a specific strategy for simulating crayfish. He uses an olive brown Wooley Bugger on a size 4, 4 x-long ring eye hook. The colors match the overall tone of many lake crayfish and the large size of the fly discourages small fish from hitting it. He uses an extra fast sinking line and a short leader with an 8 or 10 pound tippet. He uses a weedless fly if he's fishing a snaggy area.

Big trout live in the world of predator and prey, centered on two poles of existence: The need for cover and the need for food.

Float Tube Fly Fishing

He fishes ledgerock in the evening and dawn bite periods. His tactic is simple and deadly. After quietly paddling into position with his float tube, he casts his fly up into a shallow ledge area and waits 4 or 5 minutes for any fish made wary by his cast to calm down a bit. Then he retrieves the fly in quick 6-inch pulls to simulate the swimming crayfish.

Tim Tollett of Frontier Anglers, Dillon, Montana fooled this jumbo trout with a sinktip line and a No. 6 Leech.

The trick is to not retrieve too fast — just fast enough to keep the hackles and marabou pulsating. His method works because he picks out big-fish hunting territory, makes a quiet stalk, uses the right fly line, and presents the pattern properly — the undulating marabou tail and pulsating hackle drive carniverous trout crazy.

As they move towards shallow water to feed, granddaddy trout become more and more wary. Experience has taught them about diving fish-eaters like osprey, eagles, and kingfishers; any quick shadow will spook the trout back to deep water. If the fly line and leader don't line the fish, trout holding by a ledge area are particularly susceptible to flies cast up into the shallow water and worked back off the ledge.

A ploy that is especially effective for ledges and dropoffs that are irregular in shape is to retrieve the fly parallel to the fringe of the ledge. Do it so the fly climbs along the aqueous shelf but then drops off into the little underwater bays and coves. Big trout love to hover in those little pockets because they have cover and shelter but are in prime ambush position.

A tactic that is valuable whenever fishing structure adjoining deep water is to use an angled retrieve instead of the usual straight-out retrieve. Most fishermen tend to cast and retrieve the fly perpendicular to the target area. It can be much more effective to cast in at a 45 degree angle because the fly is more likely to cross in front of the trout instead of paralleling it as in a perpendicular approach.

Picture the trout heading in on a hunting territory. Older trout don't waste energy; they glide in on the feeding grounds in a fairly direct line. The standard straight-in cast is likely to line the fish or be off to the side. An angled cast presents a side-on view of the fly to the fish.

SUBMERGED ISLANDS

Submerged weedy islands are particularly rich hunting grounds for jumbo fish, especially when they adjoin deep water. Aquatic vegetation offers feed and cover to baitfish and baby trout while the additional depth of the watery ceiling over the island gives elder trout a sense of security.

Submerged islands without vegetation will often harbor crayfish, a prime big-fish staple. The lack of vegetation makes a careful approach by the fly fisherman a little more difficult, however. The most common mistake in fishing submerged islands is getting too close, usually because the angler isn't sure of the exact location of the island. By the time the structure is visible you're too close and have probably spooked the brawniest trout.

Once you've scouted out a submerged island one method for determining its location is to sight a line between two landmarks and then pick two other landmarks perpendicular to the first sight line. When you're centered at the intersection of both lines you have a way of pinpointing the spot. A topo map of the lake or reservoir and a "plumb bob depthfinder" are good tools for finding submerged islands.

WEEDBEDS

Weedbeds adjoining deep water are an outstanding big fish larder because they are one of the richest areas in a lake. Dragonfly, damselfly, mayfly, caddis, and a host of other aquatic insects inhabit weedy margins, offering food for small fish. Big trout graze on the larger insects but also favor the wee fish cruising the lush aquatic kitchen.

Concentrated hatches of mayflies, midges, or caddis or massive damselfly and dragonfly migrations or dense mayfly spinner or flying ant falls will trigger selective feeding binges by big fish. Immature trout and baitfish will feed heavily during hatches, often oblivious to the hulking trout sliding up behind them. With a quick charge the jumbo trout will attack the smaller fish, killing them in their heavy jaws.

The challenge to the fly fisher is to determine if the burly trout are feeding on insects or on the juvenile fish feeding on insects. A breeze will often create drift lanes where quantities of windblown insects accumulate, providing a concentrated feeding area. The bugs clump up, so the massive trout can inhale several at a time. Baitfish also cluster at drift lanes, offering the big predator trout a better shot at catching a prey fish off guard.

Weed Beds

Weed beds are generaly the most productive food areas of a lake because they provide forage and protection to insects as well as fish. They should be fished carefully and slowly and fly patterns experimented with until a taking pattern is found.

Gravel Shoals

Gravel shoals with aquatic vegetation and associated insect life attract minnows and are also attractive to big trout. Lake inlets and outlets support moving-water species of mayflies, caddis, and midges and are choice spawning locations. If a lake lacks an inlet or outlet, big spawners will seek out wind-aerated gravel shoals or springs percolating through gravel as redd sites.

The onset of spawning causes higher metabolic rates and distinct physical changes in mature trout. The formation of eggs or milt and aggressive courtship displays burn up more calories, triggering increased feeding. Fighting among males for females and among females for the best nesting sites lessens their natural wariness for predators.

Late spring at Henry's Lake in northeastern Idaho unlocks the cold metabolic tumblers of Henry's cutthroat trout. The cutts gradually forage more and more aggressively as their body systems revitalize. Correspondingly, aquatic creatures like leeches, scuds, freshwater shrimp, and immature nymphs of the damselfly, dragonfly, mayfly, and midge families feed and grow. The undeniable drive to search out a mate and a spawning site energizes the mature cutthroat.

At first glance Henry's Lake seems flat and featureless, captured in the serving bowl of surrounding mountains. Her flatness is a mask; the springs that feed the lake and the resultant chemical composition of her waters make Henry's Lake one of the richest trout lakes in the country.

As spawning nears, cutthroat tend to form pods of fish. In Henry's Lake they cruise out from rocky areas or gravel shorelines. Until the cutthroat begin the courtship rituals of swirling side-twisting displays, nipping and dodging rivals, fighting for a mate, and the actual redd building, they will feed and are susceptible to a fly. One way to capitalize on this nervous combative pre-spawning mood is to strip a streamer past the fish.

I cast the Zonker a comfortable double haul distance, letting the sinktip line carry the fly down a ways. The sinktip line took the fly down closer to the fish's level, but the floating portion gave me more control and kept the fly from sinking too fast, hanging up in the rocks.

I used a brisk stripping retrieve, simulating a spooked baby trout. On the fourth strip the fly was struck hard, intercepted by a heavy cutthroat. The hooked fish fought in short charging runs, punctuated by roily thrashing turns. The cutthroat didn't take out much line, but he didn't easily surrender. The big male eventually became winded, rolling heavily into the net. The cutt was a little over two hand spans long, about 18 inches, an average fish for Henry's Lake.

ADVANCED PLANNING

The linchpin for catching wary grandfather trout is a stealthy stalk. The most precise presentation and potent pattern is useless if the fish is already spooked. Noise from boats, motors, anchors, squeaky oarlocks, and oars or paddles splashing the water will scare fish — that's one of the biggest advantages of being a float tuber — you don't make any noise.

Trout are primarily visual feeders and rely on their acute eyesight to protect them from kingfishers, heron, osprey, eagles, otters, and other fish. A quick way for boaters to disperse their quarry is to stand up in the boat while flashing a graphite rod, wear bright clothes, and flail the water with repeated haphazard casts. The only pitfall for the float tuber might be in heavy-landing casts — the tuber won't spook fish because the tubing fisherman is a low-rider — the fish can't see your clothes ensemble. If you are real close to the fish they might see your flashing graphite rod, so a sidearm cast parallel to the water's surface might be a good idea.

The fly caster wanting to do battle with the biggest trout in the lake must engineer some advance planning. Recognizing prime water is necessary, but so is scouting and successful stalking. Plan out a quiet approach, figure out the optimum casting distance and angle, then determine what is the best path for the retrieved fly to take or the likeliest spot for the dry fly to intercept a cruising trout.

Part of the philosophy of advance planning is being armed with enough fly lines to effectively fish the varied mini-habitats that attract bulky trout. The lake fly fisher needs lines that match the trout's feeding depth. So the big-fish hunter not only recognizes structure but also develops a stratum strategy that melds the appropriate combination of fly and fly line to present the pattern at the trout's level in the water column.

Prime hunting grounds for big trout include snags, ledges, rock dropoffs, submerged islands, weedbeds and gravel shoals; all of these should be close to deep water.

A full floating line, Intermediate, or Intermediate sinktip are needed for dry fly fishing or fishing a subsurface presentation in the topmost layer of water.

A medium and a fast full sinking line, and a fast sinking sinktip are also necessary because of the varied types of structure that chunky trout frequent.

The most important are a full floating, a medium fast sinktip, and a medium full fast sinking line. With this selection of lines or one similar the lake fisherman is prepared to fish any lake. A shooting head setup can also be used, offering the advantages of easy distance casting and quick changeover of heads with less bulk than spare spools.

The carrousel of the seasons, the weather, and daily exchange of day for night all influence trout feeding patterns. Invariably, big trout feed best and are most receptive to the fly during the low light conditions of early morning and late evening. Water temperatures affect trout metabolic rates; water that is too cold or too hot will slow them down. Unseasonal warm weather in the spring can bring hot fishing; a midday August thunderstorm might panic baitfish and lure a lunker trout into feeding. (A fly fisherman waving a graphite rod, an excellent electrical conductor, might be wise to forego tubing during a lightning storm. I know you already know that. But big trout hunting can be a fever and the fevered often don't remember what they are doing.)

The flat surface of a lake can be difficult to read, but a modicum of detective work can shift the odds to the angler's favor. The State Department of Fish and Game or Division of Natural Resources can often provide specific information on a given lake. Biologists are usually eager to discuss seining and creel census results with interested fishermen. Fisheries population studies tell biologists not only how many trout are estimated to inhabit a lake, but also their size and just as importantly, the quantity and types of baitfish present in a lake.

Davis Lake is a fly-angling-only lake in central Oregon that has a population of large healthy rainbows, due in part to its optimum chemistry for aquatic plants and insects. But also because of its population of roach, a baitfish with an olive-gold color on its upper sides and back and a hint of silver along its lower sides.

While a group of anglers complained of poor fishing one week in July, Dick Richardson hooked a 6 pound rainbow and lost it after a 15 minute battle, landed a 4 pound fish and several small ones, 2 to 3 pounds. His stategy? Matching the predominant prey with a roach imitation of his own and Whitlock's Marabou Muddler in olive/dark yellow. The roach feed on insects among the extensive reed beds, so Dick cast his fly up into the margins of the reedy areas and let his wet tip line take his fly down. A simple stripping retrieve was all it took.

Examing shoreside spider webs for trapped insects, leeward bays for windblown bugs, sifting aquatic vegetation for nymphs, and scrutinizing stomach contents of recently caught fish will all provide clues about the probable makeup of the biomass of the lake.

In their fine book, *Lake Fishing With A Fly*, 1984, Frank Amato Publications, Ron Cordes and Randall Kaufmann list over a dozen food types and matching patterns from midges to leeches to crayfish. Because of the tremendously varied diet available to lake fish, a fly fisher can easily justify carrying hundreds of flies. Revolutionary patterns incorporating new materials like Flashabou, Flyflash, and Crystal Flash add to the lake fisherman's arsenal.

Doug Swisher loves to experiment with novel approaches and once said, "I used to catch big trout all the time in spring creeks with Zonkers and Woolly Buggers, but after awhile they didn't work as well because the trout got used to them."The same logic holds true for lakes; the fly fisher using an innovative design will often catch grandaddy trout that have rejected a multitude of standard patterns.

Old favorites can be effective, too. Once I captured a black and gray mottled dragonfly nymph in Dennis Lake, a beautiful lake set high in the Three Sisters Wilderness in the Oregon Cascades. Finding a quiet backwater I turned the nymph loose. It shot through the water, jetting with bursts of propelled water. The lesson was twofold: dragon-fly nymphs can swim quickly in fairly fast surges of speed until they regain cover and safety; and its salt-and-pepper coloration perfectly matched the volcanic lava rock surrounding the lake. When the nymph was swimming it looked just like a black Wooley Worm with grizzly hackle.

Dave Whitlock imparted a valuable tip for fishermen in his book, *Guide To Aquatic Foods*, 1982, Nick Lyons Books, when he wrote about the trout's sense of smell. He recommended rubbing a subsurface fly with moss or other aquatic vegetation to eliminate negative odors, to implant an accepted smell from the trout's environment, and to help wet the fly so it sinks better.

Undeniably, luck is an integral part of fly fishing. There is certainly nothing wrong with lucking into a big trout, but to consistently catch larger trout in lakes takes a measure of planning, proper presentation and patterns, and a strong dose of persistence. Just as the largest trout are successful predators, the big-fish fisherman also becomes a hunter. Scouting, stalking, and patience are mandatory tools for tricking the biggest trout.

Float tubes offer a high degree of accessibility. A float tuber needs only a few square feet of open area at the water's edge to launch. The small fishy-looking brushy lakes that lack boat launches, the quiet structure-riddled coves of large lakes, and pastoral farm ponds are all but a few fin strokes away. Andy Anderson photo

FOUR

ALPINE TROUT TACTICS

Backpacking for trout started for me in my late teens by borrowing my dad's work car, a 1960 Rambler with 15-inch tires, 3-speed stick on the column, and a front seat supported by a 2-by-4. The car hunkered like a giant green beetle. It handled like a truck but could transport four teenagers and their packs.

After outfitting ourselves at the Army surplus store we crammed our gear aboard and headed for the high mountains of Colorado.

Our heavy canvas packs didn't have frames, but came equipped with dozens of metal D rings and loops for attaching what didn't fit in the main compartment. With fishing poles, cups, pans, and assorted utensils hanging from every available loop and sleeping bags tied to the bottom of our packs, we looked like a band of well provisioned hoboes hiking up the trail.

We would become half orangutan, half burro, backpacking potatoes, hamburger, ketchup, eggs, bacon, bread, butter, a six-pack of Coors, cheap wine, cans of Dinty Moore beef stew, cans of soup, and cans of beans.

We sweated our way to the lake, selected a campsite, then proceeded to eat our way through our supplies.

We cooked over a smoky fire, drinking boiled coffee when we didn't spill it, and scorching our hands on too-hot pan handles. The hamburger was often only half cooked because we couldn't see in the blue smoke billowing from the fire and we were too hungry to wait, anyway.

While float tubing a mountain lake in Montana, Cutler Umbach fooled this husky West Slope cutthroat on a No. 10 Renegade.

Float Tube Fly Fishing

We opened the beans with a P-38 Army can opener and cooked them in an empty 2-pound coffee can with the lid cut off. The wire handle we installed in the coffee can cooking pot permitted us to hang it from a supporting stick over the fire. Every so often the wooden support would burn through and the pot would fall into the fire.

To supplement our provisions we would angle for brook trout. We would cast our spinning bubbles and flies out as far as we could, operating on the theory that the fish would be as far away from us as possible.

Any fish caught would be immediately cleaned and popped into a frying pan swirling with melted butter. The trout were so fresh they would curl in the pan while they cooked. Those trout taste like exotic chicken, sweet and juicy, lightly spiced with lemon pepper. We turned the trout with a spatula with a carved wooden handle, a handle whittled in between trout.

While tubing a high country lake, the author checks the spring in his 3-weight fly rod against the typical 10-inch brookie. Barbara Meyer

Some of my first fly fishing adventures consisted of stalking wary mountain brook trout in tiny streams with a nine dollar Wright and McGill Eagle Claw Favorite fiberglass fly rod. I would sneak up on the fish as best I could, then heft out the fly line, leader, and No.12 Mosquito. The store-bought flies didn't look too bad, but those first flies that I tied looked more like a No. 8 Motley Moth than a Mosquito. Fortunately, some of those brook trout didn't mind.

In the evening we smoked Wolf Bros. Crook cigars, so named because of a distinctive crook, or bend, in the cigar that allowed it to rest comfortably between the first two fingers.

The sleeping arrangement was simple: chicken-down Army surplus sleeping bags laid on a ground cover, a sheet of black plastic. Chicken-down is not a fabulous insulator; we slept with all our clothes on, jean jackets snapped tight. If it was really cold, we left our boots on, too. If it rained we rolled up in the plastic.

Chicken bags have an insidious intelligence all their own. After arranging your body around the inevitable lumps and bumps on the ground, and after some stargazing and bedside chatter, you would doze off. Before long a cagey chicken feather would work its way up your nose. A sneezing attack is the middle of the night at 10,000 feet is guaranteed to remind the camper that his whole body is stiff and sore and growing colder by the minute.

In recent years I've become a cadillac backpacker, with equipment that is lighter, more efficient, and more expensive. Modern technology has made backpacking more enjoyable because it isn't as much an ordeal. Now the only real discomfort is the actual climb itself.

I still love being in the high country in the bright summer sunshine, feasting on the sights and smells, but I hate the hard work of the climb. It is this essence of manual labor that separates out the teeming masses from the wilderness elevations. A backpacker leaves behind all the nonessentials: the excess weight of modern conveniences, the urban roar and smoke of daily life, and the elbow jostle of fellow man. Sweat from physical exercise is the coin of the realm, and even though our wilderness areas are open to all, relatively few are willing to pay the admission price.

Proper Fly and Line

Generally fish are feeding near the bottom. If casting from shallow water with a wet fly, nymph, streamer etc., match the retrieve and fly line type to the water depth.

If casting from deep water to shallow then one must continually be aware of water depth and retrieve slowly enough to keep the fly working deeply for as long as possible.

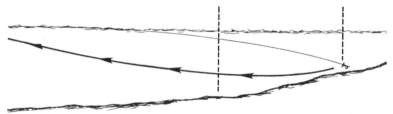

While it's true that equipment and meals need to be organized, it's even more important that the body be in shape for backpacking. A gradual program of increasingly strenuous exercise should be initiated several weeks to a month before going backpacking. Long walks, swimming, jogging, and exercises all help, and a dayhike or two before going backpacking is an excellent idea for two reasons.

The first is that a dayhike contributes to further conditioning and also acts as a barometer of physical fitness. The second reason is to provide practice at organizing needed essentials, including fishing equipment. For that reason, using the backpack for a day trip is good preparation for an overnight trip, particularly when packing in a float tube. Frequent rest periods help reduce fatigue and prevent dehydration, while the breaks provide time to enjoy the trailside scenery.

I prefer to pack in my float tube already blown up, secured with bungie cords. The tube is a bit bulky, requiring a sidestep through narrow portions of the trail, but I'm not packing the extra weight of a pump. I not only eliminate the work of pumping up the tube when I arrive at the lake, but I'm not dependent on the mechanical whims of a pump.

I remember arriving at Rainbow Lake for an evening of stalking chunky brookies up to 18 inches. Occasional rises marred the surface of the lake as my partner and I rigged our rods.The pump we brought would only fill our float tubes to about two thirds capacity − boy, that high mountain lake water was frigid sloshing in over the back of my waders. I caught a few smaller fish but the enjoyment of the trip was severely tempered by the algid bilgewater dribbling down my backside.

Reading the Rise

When a trout rises for several surface flies try to determine its direction and cast ahead of it.

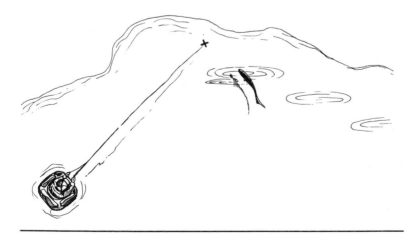

A float tube gives the angler tremendous freedom when fishing a high mountain lake. I wouldn't say that high lakes are hard to fish, but why is it that alpine lakes are invariably brushy, too boggy to wade, and generally tree-lined? Without a float tube, catching fish is only part of the challenge — the first step is getting the fly out to the fish as they cruise by just out of casting range, sipping insects only a few feet past your best cast. But to the tuber, the whole lake is readily accessible, no matter where the trout are feeding. Backpacking the additional weight of a float tube and fins is extra work, but the payoff is silent stalking and effortless casting to cruising mountain trout.

Trout Lake is a perfect example of a jewel of a backcountry lake. It's set in Oregon's Cascade Mountains in a glacier-gouged basin amidst a tumble of broken granite softened by a throng of fir and cedar clamoring for secure root space. The July sun reflects too brightly from the blue water; at the lake edges the water is so pure that it's like looking through a glass window.

In the high altitude the sun warms both terrestrial and aquatic insects quickly. The brook trout respond by easing into the shallows to browse near submerged vegetation and off ledges and snags on midge pupae, damselfly and dragonfly nymphs, and Callibaetis mayfly nymphs. Other tidbits include fallen mayfly spinners, midges returning to lay their eggs, spent dragonflies and damselflies, and myriad downed terrestrials like beetles, ants, and various other insects.

Rise rings pepper the early morning shallows of the high lake as brookies dine, supping on a varied repast. Brook trout tend to cruise when opportunist feeding, covering a territory of several square yards to perhaps whole parcels of the lake, depending on water depth, cover, and available food.

Feeding trout will trigger the twitch for any fly rodder, but a brook trout in skinny water is not an easy mark, especially from the shore. Wilderness trout stay alert for the quick shadow of a diving osprey or kingfisher, or the hunting mink or otter. Consequently, sudden movements or splashy wading or casting will scatter the wary trout.

The whole trick is to present an edible-looking fly in the brookie's cruise lane without scaring his spots off — not an easy situation from the shore of a brushy, boggy mountain lake, even with a well executed roll cast.

Ah, but the float tuber. Donning waders and flippers and slipping into his floating easy chair, he eases out from shore, finning out to the deeper water adjacent to the feeding grounds that circle the lake like a fascinating doughnut of piscine activity. Casts are snicked into the shallows with only thin air to caress the backcast.

With a little plop the forward cast drops the lightly weighted No. 16 Callibaetis Nymph only a few feet from shore, but in the danger zone of feeding brookies. The hand twist retrieve is begun with trigger tense fingers, anticipating the strike. The gentle nudge on the nymph is answered with an upraised rod and a tight line hung to an enraged brookie streaking for deeper water. The light rod bows double, snubbing the trout short of freedom. The brook trout reluctantly gives watery ground, splashing furiously on the surface.

A float tuber enjoys the closeness of the battle; being suspended in the trout's home and fighting the fish up to your lap gives the fishermen a tremendous feeling of immediate contact with the fish.

One of the big advantages of float tubing is being able to explore the whole lake. And although a lake can be hard to read at times, there are specific areas that attract feeding trout. The shallows are always a prime spot, as are ledges that drop off into deeper water, submerged weedbeds, and underwater log tangles. Floating, sinktip, and full sinking lines are needed to cover the gamut of water levels.

Water temperature and insect activity determine where the fish will feed. The hot days of summer can drive the fish deep, but most of the time trout dine in the upper water column. A full sinking line reaches fish holding deep, but a sinktip or floating line is the ticket for working the top stratum of the lake, where trout feed most of the time.

A lake fisherman can easily justify taking hundreds of flies on a trip; conditions vary tremendously from day to day and from lake to lake. One approach is to organize your flies by type. These might include: dry flies to imitate Callibaetis duns and spinners, flying ants, caddis, midges, and terrestrials like moths, beetles, wasps, and attractor flies like Humpies and Royal Wulffs; wet flies to imitate hatching mayflies, caddis, midges, damselflies, dragonflies, and various nymphs like water beetles and scuds; streamer types to simulate smaller prey fish, leeches, and crayfish; and general food type flies like the Carey Special and the Woolly Worm.

Another advantage of float tubing is that you can get within close range of the fish without spooking them because the float tube system is so quiet and the tuber presents a low silhouette in the water. Consequently, you can use the lightest of fly rods, which is even more pleasant when battling the typical 10-inch high lakes brook trout. Of course, bigger trout are all the more exciting on a light rod.

Backpacking and float tubing are both fun and when combined are a special treat. Both offer a singular kind of freedom and adventure when fly fishing a mountain lake. The sweat and work of backpacking a float tube is rewarded with unique fishing — effortless floating from a comfortable chair without a care in the world while casting to cruising trout in a crystalline alpine lake.

FIVE
FLOAT TUBING FOR
LARGEMOUTH BASS

Bass are highly efficient hide-and-seek predators. Bass migrate from deep water to the shallow recesses of their hunting territory according to the specific interplay of factors like the amount of light, water temperature, time of year, and the movements of prey.

As hunters the young bass start out feeding on micro protein like miniature freshwater shrimp and scuds and midge larvae. The bass put on weight by expanding their diet to include aquatic and terrestrial insects and bluegill, perch, and bass fry smaller than themselves.

Yearling bass are like any teenagers and are perpetually ravenous. These juvenile fish will attack anything they can get into their mouths; the shift to feeding on small bluegill and perch teaches yearling bass how to hit and swallow a fish with spiny fins − some will die from being too greedy.

Mature bass are equally opportunistic, feeding on almost any available prey, as long as its relatively big: small fish, crayfish, moths, baby snakes, mice and shrews, grasshoppers, eels, leeches, and even small birds.

Bass will strike a tremendous variety of flies providing that the artificial triggers the feeding/attack response. Fly pattern is secondary to presentation, that crucial combination of fly position and line control. Matching the fly line to the bass holding depth is vital. With an array of floating, sinktip, and full sinking lines with variable sink rates from a slow sinking Intermediate to Wet Cel II or Type II to Hi-D or Type III to Hi-Speed Hi-D or Type IV, a fly fisherman can cover almost any level in the water column.

Using a float tube to fly fish for bass is a superb way to enjoy the smaller waters overlooked by many bassmasters. Many times, the only way the lake has been fished has been from shore. That isn't the most effective way to catch bass because you should be in position out in the lake and casting in towards shore. The shore wader generally spooks far more bass than he or she catches.

The typical farm pond of several acres is superb for launching your tube to try for the biggest bass in the lake. Many of the largest bass of the season are taken from farm ponds.

The bass in most private lakes are not as sophisticated as their brethren in bigger impoundments because these smaller waters aren't constantly pounded by other fishermen. On the contrary, the bass in local ponds probably seldom see a popper or a snaky Eelworm Streamer.

ENTER THE FLY RODDER IN A FLOAT TUBE

A float tuber is a silent stalker, effortlessly gliding into position with a few strokes of the fins. The light sculling motion of the fins is under the surface and the movement of rubber underwater is perfectly quiet.

Gliding close to the bass and pond animals like muskrat, mink, and raccoons, and birds like mallards, teal, redwinged blackbirds, mourning doves and swallows without scaring them is part-and-parcel of float tubing.

Local ponds are ideal for hit-and-run fishing before and after work because the lake is close and it's so simple and easy to launch and fish from a float tube. Mornings and evenings are the best times to fly fish for bass, spring through fall. Float tubing for bass is an excellent way to start the day and an excellent way to unwind after work.

You don't need a lot of extra gear to fish for bass. Besides a floating line, you should have a sinktip and a full fast sinking line. And an extra leader and tippet material, and some floating and sinking bass flies.

Doug Swisher with a float tube fly rod bass that would be enough bucketmouth for anyone.

TACTICS

I like to start out with a floating line and a surface bug because the surface strike of a nice bass is hard to beat. Whether it's territorial aggression on the part of the bass towards a jiggling, sliding, gurgling popper or just the way of a hungry largemouth, the boiling rise of a good-sized bucketmouth is prime sport.

Sometimes you'll see a commotion back in the lily pads where a fish is working, but most of the time you're casting your bug into likely looking spots. That's the beauty of it — you never know when Mr. Big is going to bust your popper.

It's not that you're all tensed up, sculling in your floating easy chair, but pleasantly ready for action.

Providing that the fly triggers the feeding/attack response in bass, fly pattern is secondary to presentation, that crucial combination of fly position and line control.

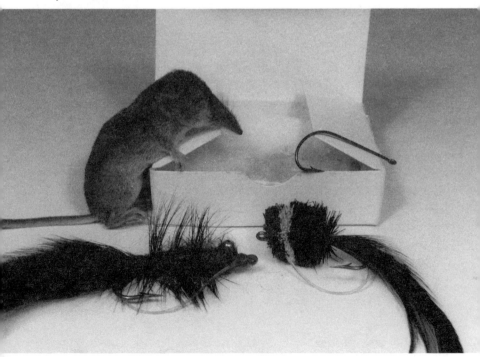

If I've fished for a bit and I know that I'm working my bug over bass but the fish just aren't willing to come to the top, I'll change tactics. I'll start working a lot of action into the popper while leaving it in one spot — tantalizing the fish by getting the rubber legs, hackle, and marabou to move as much as possible. Then if that doesn't work I'll make the bug obnoxious — spitting and splashing it's way back to me, trying to make the bass mad.

If that doesn't work I'll put on a sliding popper to slip its way up and down, while still working the top layer of the water column. If the bass still won't move I'll go to a subsurface fly but still use a floating line, particularly in the shallows where the bass are most likely to be in a feeding mood.

Once you move out of the shallows, you need to employ sinktip and full sinking lines to send your fly down to where the fish are holding. An excellent tactic is to rein in your float tube out a ways from structure that adjoins deeper water, then cast in towards the shallow water where it joins the deeper water, like at creek mouths, reed islands, old submerged riverbeds or roads, or any other type of bass-holding structure.

Then use a sinktip or full sinking line with a subsurface fly like a Whitlock Eelworm Streamer and cast up to the shallows, and retrieve your fly so that it follows the bottom contour out to your float tube. It's a deadly tactic, particularly if you get the fly all the way to the bottom and keep it there and yet still maintain contact with the fly to detect the bass picking up your fly. Sometimes they will hit it hard, but often they will just pick up the fly or run a little ways with it — it transmits up the fly line in a real subtle manner — detecting the strike requires concentration.

TIPS FOR CATCHING MORE BASS

One way to increase your chances for a hookup is to keep your rod low to the water and when a bass strikes, snap the rod up but keep your wrist and arm straight, giving the hook the maximum power, sinking the hook into the bass's bony mouth. Using Tiemco 8089 or Mustad 37187 Stinger hooks will help; they were designed specifically for bass fishing.

A graphite rod is the most sensitive and is an advantage when fishing the subsurface fly. Some anglers will dip the front third of the rod underwater when fishing the sunken fly, pointing the rod right at the fly. This lessens the friction between you and your fly and gives you a straight path for detecting the strike.

The fly pattern that you use is of secondary importance to the way you show it to the fish. The fly must be at the proper depth; it must be where the bass are feeding or resting in ambush cover. The fly should have lots of built-in movement; a stiff fly doesn't work nearly as well as one with rubber legs, soft hackle, marabou, or Crystal Flash. And lastly, the fly should be manipulated so that the fly moves as much as possible while staying in one spot.

You can impart movement to your fly with light tugs on the line. You can lift or lower the rod, but controlling the line without moving the rod gives you the advantage of being in constant contact with your fly. When you move your rod you lose some of your direct contact with the fly, especially when the rod is being lowered after you've raised it. Some of the sensitivity is lost while the rod is in motion.

When you do begin retrieving the fly you can deliver various fish-enticing retrieves. Some of the best are pull-and-pause retrieves, which give the bass a chance to follow its prey while still staying close to cover. Often, if you can get the fish to move even a few inches, your chances of hooking that bass are greatly improved.

Incorporating a pause in the retrieve gives you the chance to give the fly little twitches while the fly is stopped, which drives bass crazy. The straight same-speed retrieves will sometimes work when pause-type retrieves won't, and the trick here is to try different speeds of retrieve. Some days an extremely slow but steady retrieve is the ticket and some days an extremely fast retrieve is what it takes to excite the bass.

Experimenting with retrieves can often make a big difference in how many fish you catch.

The most common mistake fishermen make when fly fishing for bass is working their bugs too fast. In most cases the bass want to inspect that fly, sometimes for a minute or longer. Sixty seconds can be a long time to the intense fly fisherman. The fly rodder has a distinct advantage when the bass are slow to strike because a fly has all those easily-moved built-in parts that respond to the slightest little stir in the fly line. A bass fly has more built-in animation than a stiff plastic plug.

Fan Casting

The float tube allows fan casting left to right or vice versa as you read the water's surface for a hint of what is happening below.

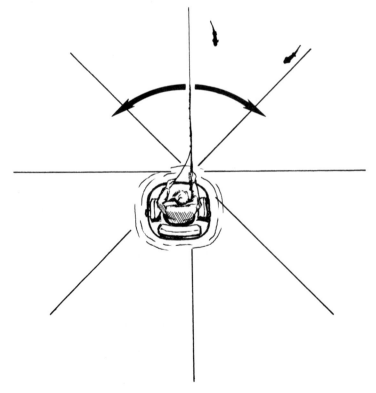

JOYS OF FLOAT TUBING FOR BASS

Part of the enjoyment of float tubing for bass is being suspended in their world. You are finning in the same water they are finning in. And since you are so close to their underwater arena, the sounds, smells, and sights zoom you into tight focus with the bass. You sense much of what the bass senses; the only way to get closer is to be underwater with the fish.

Another part of the fun of float tubing is when you hook a bass, battling the fish right up to you. When the bass jumps, gills rattling, that fish is eye-level to the float tuber, practically in the float tuber's lap. It's great. You feel like part of the pond, part of the bass's world – even though the fish is mad at being hooked and you're chuckling like an idiot in your float tube. And you don't bend over to get your fish – you lip-lock that bass right in front of you, practically in your pocket.

And even though many bass live in grungy waters, most farm ponds and many lakes are fairly clear with banks canopied with lush vegetation and a variety of interesting structure to cast to. In all likelihood, no one else is flyfishing the lake. The classic pastoral farm pond is almost always deserted, the quiet calm interrupted only by splashes of feeding largemouth. A perfect place to float tube.

More and more bass fishermen are going catch-and-release. Just as with any other prized gamefish, bass can't hold up to the increased pressure of more and more fishermen, so most bass fishermen are limiting their kill and turning loose the bigger fish. And even though a small farm pond may not get the pressure of a more popular lake, it still makes sense to restrict your kill. It makes particularly good sense to turn loose the big fish because those are your choice spawning fish and by killing them you may be harming your fishery. Why not have the thrill of catching that big hog over and over instead of just once?

SIX

NEUTRAL DENSITY BASS FLIES

Baitfish don't necessarily behave like most flies do. Fish don't float to the top or sink to the bottom, as flies do. The majority of the time baitfish are suspended. They tend to hover at whatever depth they are in at the time.

Neutral density bass plugs are designed to neither sink nor float. When the retrieve is stopped the plug stays at the same depth, simulating characteristic baitfish behavior.

Bass flies can also be designed to act as neutral density prey. The chief advantage to a neutral density fly is that the fly will stay at the same depth on the retrieve and allow for a very slow retrieve without the fly sinking below the desired depth or popping to the surface. When a pause is inserted into the retrieve, the fly will hover. A motionless suspended baitfish that merely twitches is irresistible to predatory bass.

Depth is controlled by fly line sink rate. Once the retrieve is started the correct density sinking fly line won't sink any deeper. Nor will the fly, because the fly is tied so that the weight of the materials used is offset by built-in floatation.

The basic ingredients for tying a neutral density or hover fly can be applied to a variety of bass prototype patterns: baitfish simulators; baby bluegill, perch, and bass; undulating leeches; swimming snakes and eels; and a host of other creatures.

Compared to the built-in movement factor of a bass fly, a plastic plug is like a stiff stick. Plugs require a retrieve to impart a semblance of life-like prey movement. Even though the fly may be at rest underwater, it's hackle, tail, legs, and wings are still vacillating. Consequently, a bass fly can be far more responsive to subtle line handling than a plug.

So the first ingredients for a good hover fly are materials that are soft and flexible, materials that wiggle easily when wet. These include marabou, rubber legs, soft hackle (like hen chicken, grouse, and pheasant), and rabbit fur strips.

Flashabou and Crystal Flash are excellent materials because they are soft and flexible, and give off quick sparkles of reflected light which are similar to the sparkles of silver-sided baitfish. But just as importantly, the bright flashes attract bass by igniting an excited curiosity. Crystal Flash is narrow strands of twisted flashabou that give off sparkles of reflected light no matter which direction the fly is turned. Crystal Flash reflects more light and moves more easily in the water. Flashabou is better if more bulk in the fly is desired.

Flashabou tubing is ideal for the body. Wire ribbing adds strength to the fly body and doll eyes or bead eyes help simulate the predominate eyes of bass prey. Hover flies are tied on Stinger hooks, Tiemco 8089 or Mustad 37187, most often with a weed guard and in a variety of colors and patterns.

Most deadly subsurface bass flies that have become standards, like the Eelworm Streamer, can be adapted to perform as neutral density flies by incorporating the main ingredient — a built-in floatation chamber.

Closed cell foam is the ticket; ensolite used for sleeping pads is excellent for tying hover flies. Neutral density flies require more fiddling around because it can't be accurately determined beforehand whether the floatation of the foam will offset the tendency of the fly to sink from its total weight. A certain amount of experimentation is required. A hover fly can be tested for floatation in the bathroom sink. The fly must be thoroughly wet and held underwater to see what it will do. Some will hover, but some will have a neutral-minus or neutral-plus floatation. Those will either slowly sink or rise to the surface. They are fishable as is, or may be modified.

If that fly sinks, when you tie the next one you can use more ensolite or use less or the water-absorbing materials (like hackle or fur) or reduce the overall weight of the fly by eliminating the bead eyes or use a thread rib instead of wire. If the fly floats to the top, you can add a small amount of lead wire to the fly at the head or the tail. You can gain consistency by practicing with the same pattern on the same size hook.

Fishing a neutral density fly gives the angler the advantage of knowing that the fly is at the same level as the fly line. Traditional bass streamers tend to sink below or rise above the level of the fly line, a disadvantage when the fisherman is working a specific holding level. A delicate strike is more readily detected when the fly is in a direct line with the fly line, and setting the hook is more positive because of the direct line of pull.

Hover flies are particularly effective when the bass are suspended at a specific depth and are reluctant to feed at any other level. The angler can exploit that holding station with a neutral density fly because the fly will stay at that depth. With the proper sinking line, subtle variations of retrieve can be added. Pauses, quick jerks of the line which cause the fly to quiver, start-and-stop retrieves, and other inventive modifications can be included into the presentation of the fly.

Because the neutral density fly is hovering, the fisherman can impart a patient tantalizing life-like mobility to a fly that actually isn't moving very far. Most importantly, the fly doesn't sink below the strike zone, but continually tugs at the bass attack trigger.

Neutral density flies are certainly not the answer to all the field problems of bass fly fishing, and even though hover flies require more messing around at the tying bench, they add another important tactic to fly fishing for bass.

BASSABOU MATUKA-Deke Meyer
A neutral density fly prototype

Varied overall color schemes: *purple, black, electric blue, brown, olive, bright green, yellow*
Hook: Tiemco 8089 or Mustad 37187 Stinger, No. 10 to 1/0
Thread: Kevlar, monocord, Nymo, or other heavy thread
Tail: Marabou sandwiched with strips of Flashabou or Crystal Flash
Underbody: Closed cell ensolite
Body: Flashabou tubing
Wing: Dyed rabbit strip
Rib: Wire
Hackle: Dyed webby saddle hackle
Snag Guard: .020 or .025 inch stiff monofilament (25 or 30-lb. Maxima)
Eyes: Doll eyes

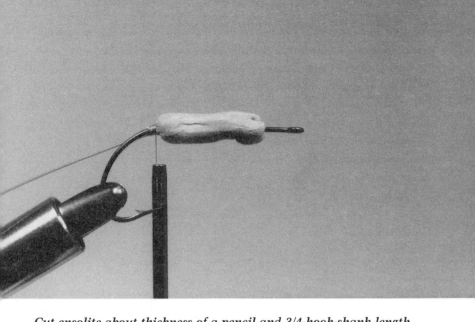

Cut ensolite about thickness of a pencil and 3/4-hook-shank length. Push hook through ensolite point-first and put hook in vise. Attach thread at rear of hook, tie down ensolite at rear and tie in mono snag guard.

Tie in marabou tail, wire rib, and flashabou or crystal flash. (Flashabou and crystal flash handle easier if moistened.)

Remove core from flashabou tubing. Slip tubing over ensolite and tie at rear. Whip finish thread, trim, and cement. (The tubing is tied in so that strands of flashabou trail out to the rear with the marabou tail.)

Thread is reattached at the front of the hook. Ensolite, tubing, and rabbit strip are tied down.

Wire ribbing is brought forward through the rabbit and tied down. (A bodkin or needle is helpful for separating the fur as the wire is brought forward.) Bring the snag guard up and tie off and trim so the guard loop is a little bigger than the hook gape.

Tie in the front hackle collar, wrap it wet fly style, so the hackle points to the rear, tie off and trim. Tie in lead eyes or bead eyes, glue on doll eyes or paint on eyes. Whip finish and cement head.

SEVEN
FLOAT TUBING FOR SMALLMOUTH BASS

Lake dwelling smallmouth are an ideal fly rod quarry because they feed in close to shore during much of the spring, summer, and fall months. And the tackle needed for smallmouth is lighter than what is used for largemouth bass, making it all the more enjoyable.

Smallmouth are strong fighters, bending 6 and 7 weight fly rods as if the smallmouth were a much heavier fish. Smallmouth always seem much bigger until you land them; like trout they average 10 to 14 inches. That sounds like a paltry fish, but a smallmouth is a tight compact bundle of muscular energy, digging into the water like a high-powered mole. These scrappers don't give up until they are pulled completely out of the water. Even when you finally get one to come up, the smallmouth is liable to bust out on top of the water in swirling splashes. They are fun. And of course, there is always the chance of catching the bigger 17 to 19 inch smallmouth, or the dream fish over 20 inches.

According to the International Game Fish Association, the

all-tackle record for smallmouth was an 11 pound 15 ounce fish taken from Deep Hollow Lake, Kentucky, in 1955 by David Hayes. That almost-12 pound smallmouth is bigger than any record smallmouth taken in the last 30 years. The closest is a 10 pound 8 ounce fish from Hendricks Creek, Kentucky, caught by Paul Beal on 8 pound class line in 1986.

All the current IGFA freshwater line class records for smallmouth were set between 1983 and 1986. That same trend holds true for most of the records for most of the species of fish recognized by the IGFA. It appears that anglers are getting better at catching bigger fish. Currently, the biggest fly rod record smallmouth is a 4 pound 6 ounce fish from James River, Snowden, Virginia, caught by Noel Burkhead on 12 pound class line in 1985. I'm certain that new fly rod records for smallmouth will be set as more fly fishermen pursue smallmouth, particularly from a float tube.

Some pristine northern lakes are famous for topwater smallmouth fishing with poppers. It requires ideal conditions: a lake with clear water, a good population of smallmouth, and minimal disturbance from power boats. The traditional way to fish poppers for smallmouth is from a canoe, but float tubing is also a great way to fish topwater for smallmouth, particularly if you know where some fish are feeding close to the surface.

Smallmouth are most likely to smack surface poppers when the fish are holding in less than 6 feet of water and the water temperature is above 60 degrees. Although smallmouth prosper in cooler waters than largemouth, their preferred range of water temperature is still from 65 to 71 degrees, as compared to 68 to 75 degrees for largemouth bass.

Some smallmouth lakes host populations of the big Yellow Mayfly (Hexagenia limbata). This mayfly is equivalent to a size 6 dry fly, so big Wulff-type dries work well during the hatch. An emergent pattern, like a Wooley Worm or a large Soft Hackle that imitates the hatching Yellow May nymph is also effective, particularly if windblown waves obscure the dry fly from the fish.

However, in most lakes and reservoirs, the best way to

catch smallmouth is subsurface because the smallmouth feed primarily on underwater prey. Like all bass, a smallmouth will eat almost anything it can get into its mouth. But the two main diet staples are crayfish and smaller fish. So it behooves the fly fisher to imitate crayfish or prey fish in pattern and presentation.

The best float tubing spots for smallmouth are similar in specific characteristics for any smallmouth lake. There are several favorite smallmouth feeding areas that are ideal for the float tuber. In early spring the grassy slopes that edge off into the lake will attract fish because they heat up a little earlier and will hold baby baitfish feeding on the insects in the aquatic vegetation. Drift lanes that attract small fish that feed on windblown insects are alluring to smallmouth, particularly if there is cover available, like pods of reeds or submerged rocky caverns.

Another good bet is sunken structure that is 4 to 6 feet underwater like rock ledges, and submerged gravel-covered islands or gravel patches surrounded by reeds or other aquatic plants. It's speculated that smallmouth are attracted to rocky or gravel areas because of the higher numbers of crayfish and nymphs that live in the rubble. Smallmouth feed on the crayfish, the bigger aquatic insects, and the small fish also feeding on the nymphs. In addition, biologists know that when in the spring water temperatures reach 62 to 65 degrees, smallmouth spawn in rocky gravel areas.

The best all-around hot spots for smallmouth are the rocky points that slant off into deep water. Smallmouth just love gravel or rocky bottom structure, especially when they share it with crayfish. When the surface is calm, a float tuber can fish any structure in the lake, but when the wind comes up, float tubers head for safe fiords and fish the outcroppings protected from the wind. The ideal combination is a series of rocky points within a secure cove or bay that is protected from the wind and heavy waves.

The most consistent depth for catching smallmouth on a fly rod is when the fish are in less than 10 feet of water. A fast sinking line will be your main gun most of the time, because the fish will be holding in close to the rocks on the bottom.

And because the fly will be just above or right in the rocks, a weedless design is the most effective. Keel hooks are particularly effective when the fly is probing the rocky depths of smallmouth cover. The smallmouth fishermen should be armed with a large number of flies and a good hook hone because the fly must be retrieved from in and around the rocky cover that smallmouth prefer, and you will lose flies. Fortunately, smallmouth flies are quick and easy to tie. Simulation of food prey is more important than specific realistic imitation of antennae, legs, or forearm joints on smallmouth flies.

Some good smallmouth flies include Wooley Worms, Zonkers, Marabou Streamers, Fur Strip Leeches, and simple crayfish patterns in sizes 4 to 8. Many trout fishermen already have suitable smallmouth patterns in their trout fly collection. Trout also feed on small fish, nymphs, and crayfish. But most trout fishermen dislike probing snaggy areas with their flies and consequently, will miss out on some first rate smallmouth fishing.

The shoreline of Lake Billy Chinook in central Oregon is formed from flooded ancient river canyons that once cut through jumbled blocks of volcanic rock. Denise Trobridge has hooked a smallmouth with a full sinking line and a No. 6 crawfish fly worked along the bottom.

Float Tube Fly Fishing

Obviously, catching a smallmouth is one way to find out if there are fish in any particular spot. So the fly rodder actually tries to do three things at once: find out where the fish are holding, discover which fly will work, and determine which retrieve is effective, all by catching that first fish of the day.

Unless you always fish warm water or don't get cold easily, neoprene stockingfoot waders are the best for float tubing. Andy Anderson photo

So the float tubing fly rodder launches with a creelful of hunches, advice, and previous experience, but catches fish by experimentation and persistence. The biggest problem is finding the fish. But that is often the case, no matter what fish you are pursuing in any given lake.

Information from tackle shop personnel or fishermen returning from hunting smallmouth can clue you in on potential hot spots. Often, fishermen will be looking for trout or landlocked salmon or largemouth bass and will catch smallmouth. That's ok, it adds to your pool of knowledge about the smallmouth — it can give you some valuable leads about where the smallies are holding or just as importantly, where they aren't feeding.

Members of the local bass club can be a big help in locating smallmouth waters and in giving advice about specific spots to fish a lake, especially the shallower zones that might be float tube fly rod country. Shallow is a relative term, however, as a bassmaster in his bass boat may consider 15 to 20 feet as shallow water if he's been fishing in 40 feet of water.

The fly rodder will do better in waters of less than 10 feet because of the relatively slow rate of sink for even an extra-fast sinking line and weighted fly in comparison to conventional rods loaded with monofilament and a weighted jig. And by the time you begin the retrieve, because of the 45 degree angle that the fly tracks from your tube, you only get about 2/3 of the distance cast as the fishable retrieve. For example, if you cast 45 feet out and your fly sinks down 8 or 9 feet, your fishable retrieve is only about 25 feet long. No, a fly rod setup isn't as efficient as a flipping'stick and a level-wind baitcasting reel, but it can be great fun.

LAKE BILLY CHINOOK SMALLMOUTH BASS

Lake Billy Chinook in central Oregon is typical of many northern reservoirs in that its waters are cold enough for salmonids like trout and kokanee salmon and yet warm enough to support a vigorous population of smallmouth bass. The smallmouth in Lake Billy Chinook are slow growing but get up over four pounds. The current Oregon state record is a 6 pound 13 ounce fish from the Powder River, caught by Mark Weir on June 1, 1978.

Lake Billy Chinook was formed by Round Butte Dam, built in 1963 for generating electricity. The reservoir was named by the Confederated Tribes of the Warm Springs Indian Reservation in honor of a 19 year old Chinook Indian, who accompanied John C. Fremont on his explorations of central Oregon in 1843.

Fremont was only 30 years old when he trekked along the Deschutes River, heading south to California. He eventually led five expeditions across the western United States, was for several weeks a U.S. Senator for California, was nominated for the Republican party as President in 1856, was a major-general in the Civil War, and was a railroad president. He is chiefly remembered for his first three exploring expeditions across the western states.

Lake Billy Chinook was formed by damming three rivers: the Deschutes, the Metolius, and Crooked Rivers. Over the eons, these rivers have cut immense canyons through layers of volcanic rock, ash, and ancient lava flows.

The backbone of the Cascade mountains to the west of Lake Billy Chinook is a chain of volcanoes of relatively recent geologic vintage. Mount St. Helens, only about 200 miles northwest of the lake, blew up on May 18, 1980.

In his narratives about his expedition in 1843, when in the present-day town of The Dalles, Oregon, Fremont wrote, "On the 23rd of the preceding November (1842), St. Helens had scattered ashes like a white fall of snow, over The Dalles of the Columbia, 50 miles distant. A specimen of these ashes was given to me by Mr. Brewer, one of the clergymen at The Dalles."

The town of The Dalles lies about 100 miles due north of Lake Billy Chinook, which is just west of Madras, Oregon.

This is the shape of Lake Billy Chinook: a reservoir of clear blue-green water that is shaped like a three-fingered hand with a very short palm; the fingers are formed by each of the three river channels while the palm holds 400-foot high Round Butte Dam.

Smallmouth are a tight compact bundle of muscular energy; when hooked they dig into the water like a high-powered mole. Because they feed in close to shore during much of the season, lake dwelling smallmouth are an ideal float tube quarry.

But the flavor of the reservoir is just as significant: the deep river canyons gouged from the volcanic shruggings of the Cascades are striated with layers of geologic history that overlook the reservoir. In fact, the volcanic debris is part of the lake itself: jumbled blocks of volcanic rock flung from the mouth of ancient fire cones comprise the steep portions of most of the shoreline of the reservoir; volcanic pumice and ash are layered to form a few sloping beaches.

Indian petroglyphs are etched in rock, and prehistoric fossil remains of trees, fish, camels, three-toed ponies, and short-legged rhinos are captured in between the layers of basalt and ash that form the canyon walls.

The country is drab: the scattered juniper and scrub oak are pale olive; and the canyons and rock formations are muted shades of gray, tan, and light brown.

The distance the fly is actually on the bottom of the lake during the retrieve equals only about two-thirds the total distance of the cast.

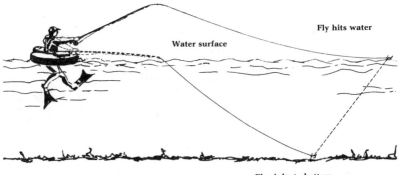

Water surface

Fly hits water

Fly sinks to bottom.

Lake Billy Chinook is a good float tubing reservoir because of the various coves and inlets that protect the float tuber from the wind. Wind is common on the lake, building up waves on the main body of water that make it hard to propel the tube, hard to stay in casting position, and hard to detect a strike to the retrieved fly.

Inflatable rubber floating contraptions are not new – during his 1843 expedition, Fremont used an 18 foot long inflatable rubber boat built along the lines of a birchbark canoe to navigate across many of the rivers. (The fishing was so bad on the Bear River on August 28, 1843, that Fremont's party was skunked in the classic sense – they ate a skunk for dinner.)

Lake Billy Chinook has a tremendous population of crayfish; the smallmouth also feed on juvenile squawfish, suckers, trout, and both baby largemouth and smallmouth bass. According to Oregon Department of Fish & Wildlife electroshocking and creel census statistics, the smallmouth bass population outnumbers the largemouth by a factor of 10 to 1.

Just like everywhere else, the key to catching smallmouth is finding the fish. The coves and inlets have rocky points and some have grassy areas that hold fish. Once the holding pattern of the fish has been discovered, then the games begin.

When Denise Trowbridge and I fished Lake Billy Chinook one September, the bass were holding in 6 to 8 feet of water off two types of structure: the classic rocky point adjoining deep water; and a rocky bluff stitched with a half submerged fallen tree.

Denise used a 9 foot graphite rod matched with a fast-sinking 7 weight line and a No. 6 Crayfish fly tied on a conventional hook. The fly pattern was simple: brown chenille body weighted in front to give the fly a jigging action, palmered brownish yellow grizzly hackle, and two pair of brownish yellow grizzly hackle tips flared outward to suggest crayfish pincers.

I used a 9 1/2 foot graphite rod matched with a fast-sinking 6 weight line and a No. 6 Keel Black and Grizzly Wooley Bugger. We both caught smallmouth and we both got hung up on the bottom. I like to think that the keel hook was less snag prone, but I was concentrating on catching fish, not counting snags. Even with the fly tied on a keel hook, every so often I had to fin over and work the fly loose from the rocks. We caught enough fish to make it fun. Not hot and heavy action, but we caught smallmouth.

Denise never did return my Crayfish fly; said she wanted to use it as a pattern. I was amazed that she could fish it through smallmouth cover and even though it snagged up, she never lost the fly. She just kept sharpening the hook and yanking smallmouth.

At one point, Denise and I had both just released nice smallmouth, had recast, and were concentrating on probing sunken cover from the best angle when I got another strike.

I set the hook and felt solid resistance. The fish bucked and then ran 20 feet out toward deeper water. The fly rod bent deeply from the power of the husky fish.

"This is a good one," I yelled over to Denise.

"That's great," she answered vaguely, concentrating on her own fly.

I gradually worked the fish close to the surface. It rolled briefly and I saw a flash of gold and a fish body about 20 inches long.

"This is a whopper," I yelled, "It could go four pounds or better."

As I led the fish in, it showed its true coloration and form — it was over 20 inches all right, but it was a massive squawfish. Squawfish are native to these waters but are considered a trash fish because they are too bony to eat and often go limp after one strong run.

"Damn, it's only a squawfish," I told Denise.

"Well, at least it's a nice one," she chuckled.

THE FUTURE: MORE SMALLMOUTH FROM FLOAT TUBES

I predict that more and more fly fishermen will try smallmouth from a float tube, especially since modern float tubes are not only comfortable but have extra pockets and cushy backrests. In addition, neoprene waders keep the float tuber warm in the often chilly waters of the best smallmouth lakes.

Except under ideal conditions, the open reaches of our biggest reservoirs and lakes are not for the float tuber. However, the float tuber can explore the little coves and bays that are out of the way of power boats and water skiers.

The chief challenge lies in locating the fish, but rocky points and grassy reefs and weedlines are fairly consistent producers, especially in wind-protected bays, because that's where the crayfish live and small prey fish feed on nymphs.

The successful smallmouth fisherman will be the one who concentrates on presenting the fly where the smallmouth are; water depth, water temperature, and holding cover are the key factors – not fly pattern. It's much more important to have a buggy looking fly at the right spot than an exact replica of a crayfish or baby baitfish that the fisherman is afraid of losing to a snag because he spent so much time tying the fly.

When fishing for predatory gamefish is slow, you can try a salt water style of retrieve — pin your rod under your elbow and use both hands to strip in the fly — a fast moving streamer will often attract the largest fish.

EIGHT
FLOAT TUBING
FOR BLUEGILL

Spring is synonymous with fly fishing for bluegill. With the sunny days and warming water, bluegill begin cruising the shallows, snacking on diverse tidbits in the aquatic larder like damselfly and dragonfly nymphs, Callibaetis mayfly nymphs, and most importantly, Chironomid midges. Once the pond is warm enough to stir increased metabolic activity, springtime bluegill become ravenous, inhaling any available mouth-sized food. The bluegill's penchant for vigorous spring feeding and nest building makes them an ideal early season fly rod quarry, especially with a light rod. Light gear, simple patterns, and simplistic techniques are the perfect antidote for the winter-crazed fly rodder.

I'm drawn to bluegill ponds as surely as a magnet draws iron. My earliest fishing expeditions started with rolling my blue bicycle with its 24-inch balloon tires out of the garage and down the early summer morning street. The wire basket on the front of the bike carried the cloth creel, which was also the tackle bag and lunch stash. My metal telescopic rod had three guides and a creaky reel loaded with 25-pound test black dacron line. It was secured parallel to the handlebars by my locked thumbs. There is no cleaner sweat than that of a furiously pedalling nine-year-old caught up in youth's exuberance to go fishing.

My boyhood bluegill pond was a two-mile ride, punctuated in the end by scrambling ankle-high tennis shoes and an arm or two of rod and all-purpose creel. A bright red Prince Albert can was fiddled out of the bag and a wriggling worn entrained on the hook. A stalwart elm tree had provided a great branch that swooped out over the pond, the perfect bluegill dapping bulwark.

The striated red worms pirated from my mother's garden compost pile would squirm their way through the duckweed to meet their destiny in the clamped jaws of a hungry bluegill. Many a 'gill was brusquely yarded up through the tree branches and dumped into the creel. Our cats ate like kings.

The spring song of the red-winged blackbird and the busy putterings of mallards permanently embossed my memory. Perhaps the dodging of yard work and desperate flight from my mother's spring cleaning program are what made those early fishing trips so memorable. But I doubt it. I fish for bluegill simply because it's fun and still immensely gratifying.

One of the reasons fly fishing for bluegill is so enjoyable is that the lightest fly rods match the fish and the fishing. By using a 2, 3, or 4 weight outfit, the dueling might of the fish is greatly increased. As the bluegill turns its flat body sideways, its staunch surges are forcefully transmitted up a light rod — in essence, the fighting power of the fish is greatly magnified.

Another reason for using a light rod is that most casts for bluegill are under 40 feet. The average cast is about 25 to 30 feet, the perfect range for a 2 to 4 weight rig.

Besides which, smaller trout flies work just fine for bluegill and can be cast easily with a light rod and line. As well as being a joy in itself, fly fishing for bluegill in the spring is an excellent tuneup for trout season. You can hone your casting, resharpen your timing for setting the hook, and enjoy fly fishing after a long winter. You may also discover that your tippet material is low or that you're almost out of dry fly floatant. Better at the bluegill pond than during a hatch matched by rising rainbow.

One spring I put two bluegill in an aquarium to observe their feeding habits. The first thing that struck me was how beautiful bluegill are; their muted overall coloration replicates the somber browns and greens of their underwater habitat, while their aqua-blue cheeks and yellow-orange underbellies are a startling contrast.

What impressed me most was the translucency of their front fins, the pectorals. Because fish are opaque, no fish is actually translucent, but bonefish, browns, and bluegill take on a translucid quality because of the interaction between sunlight, water, and camouflaging.

Bluegill pectorals are slim, lightly spotted, and mirror the background; the result is a translucent effect. As the bluegill swims, the pectorals are like underwater butterflies lightly steering this way and that.

Bluegill are exquisite on a light fly rod; by using a 2, 3, or 4-weight outfit the dueling power of the bluegill is greatly magnified.

A bluegill is built like a bulgy plate. Bluegill are designed to slide in and out of reeds, aquatic plants, and tangles of submerged brush and tree limbs. Because of its shape a trout would be totally inefficient in the bluegill's world; a trout swims the more open water of lakes and streams while the bluegill lances in and out of the lacery of underwater cover.

A bluegill feeds by gliding up behind prey and inhaling it, swallowing its food and a mouthful of water at the same time. But a bluegill has a dainty mouth, limiting the size of its prey.

Watching a bluegill feed in an aquarium is akin to watching a kid suck a milkshake with a straw. If a bluegill mouth can be said to pucker, bluegill suck in their nymphs, worms, and tadpoles in much the same way as we vacuum up a chocolate shake.

When fishing for bluegill, strikes to a sunken fly can be hard to detect because the fish merely sucks the fly into its small mouth. In the aquarium the bluegill would move up right behind its prey and swallow it, while the food would only move just a fraction of an inch. Those millimeters of movement don't telegraph well up a leader and fly line.

When surface feeding, bluegill have more in common with the Rocky Mountain whitefish than trout or bass. When a bluegill takes a surface insect, the fisherman often hears a distinctive pop because the fish is sucking the insect and some water held by a certain amount of surface tension, into its little mouth.

Rocky Mountain whitefish also have a small mouth. When whitefish rise the mechanics are much the same and often result in a popping sound that is specific to whitefish. Although a trout or a bass can create quite a disturbance when it rises, their mouth is large enough to eliminate the popping sound.

FLOAT TUBE BLUEGILL

Fly fishing for bluegill from a float tube is the embodiment of simplicity.

Float Tube Fly Fishing

A float tube opens a treasure chest of angling mobility. The brushy marshy shallows that bluegill like so well can be fished from the comfort of a float tube, without crashing around on shore, wading in and out of the muck of most ponds. A hooked fish can be fought out in the open, in lieu of dragging it through the shoreline cattails. And you will land more of the bigger bluegill because they won't be able to bury themselves in the shoreline snags.

Since the float tuber only needs a few square feet of clear ground to launch, the tuber can fish the brushy ponds that boaters and bank waders avoid. Many of those overlooked ponds harbor the biggest bluegill.

A float tube functions much like an aquatic zoom lens, bringing the fisherman into close focus with the aqueous world of bluegill, bustling nymphs, and the fascinating laceries of underwater plants.

Big bluegill are the elite — they have successfully nourished themselves without being eaten.

One day I was tubing a favorite pond, catching bluegill on a size 16 Soft Hackle Nymph, listening to the call of a pair of mourning doves in a dead oak tree and the challenge of a male redwinged blackbird. Some adult midges were flying here and there but I had only seen a few sporadic surface rises.

From my heron-like vantage point in the tube I saw an adult midge hit the water's surface two feet away. The insect hit the water hard enough to break the surface tension and begin swimming down until she was out of sight. Shortly she reappeared, swimming strongly upward until she broke the surface film and flew away. Watching her underwater locomotion was fascinating in itself, but the silvery sheen of the air bubble enclosed under her wings was even more intriguing.

In W. Patrick McCafferty's book, *Aquatic Entomology*, Science Books International, 1981, he says of midges "Females oviposit directly on the water, on submerged substrate, on shoreline substrate, or on aquatic vegetation, depending on the species." Of the air bubble he says, "Dense coverings of microscopic, unwettable hairs or scales hold the bubble or layer of air to the insect's body while submerged. The film of air held in such a manner is called a plastron."

For the fisherman, the midge's diving behavior and the plastronic breathing setup explain the bluegill's attraction to the Soft Hackle fly, a pattern with the light-reflective sparkle of fine wire or tinsel and the movement of hackle fibers. Fishing from the perspective of a float tube allowed me to eavesdrop on a tantalizing glimpse into the daily happenings under the watery curtain of a bluegill pond.

WET FLY BLUEGILL

The Soft Hackle Nymph is easy and inexpensive to tie. It has the built-in movement of soft hackles, a rough-dubbed body to suggest the indistinct outline of most underwater insects, a little sparkle of light-reflecting wire, and is a good generalist pattern for simulating many kinds of subsurface aquatic insects. Soft hackle is any kind of hackle that is soft and webby, allowing it to soak up water easily and ripple enticingly in response to the slightest motions from the fly rod or line. Good soft hackles are found on hen chickens and upland game birds like pheasant, quail, grouse, chukar, or partridge. A few fibers are sufficient for the tail of the Soft Hackle Nymph. Some of the smaller hackles can be wound for the front hackle on the nymph. Bigger feathers can be tied in so just the tip of the hackle is wound on or they can be tied on in little bunches so you can adjust the hackle length to trail back about half the body length of the fly.

A rough-dubbed body is one that has the guard hairs of the fur included; the little spicules of hair can suggest gills or legs or projecting setae of aquatic insects and imply life and movement. One approach is to mix easily dubbed fur like rabbit, beaver, or Australian opposum with the coarser hair from mink, otter, woodchuck, or coyote. The dubbing can be spun on the fly with the aid of a sticky wax on the thread. Moistening the fingers helps, too. The noodle method of spinning the fur with a loop of tying thread, originated by Polly Rosborough, makes a nice tight fly.

Overall coloration of most insects is in the earthtone shades of brown, tan, gray, and black, which suggests using the same subtle colors for the Soft Hackle Nymph. For example, use mottled brown grouse for the tail fibers and the front hackle and dub a brown rabbit/mink body ribbed with fine copper wire. Besides adding sparkle, the wire ribbing reinforces the body so the fly will last longer. An underbody of lead wire will help the nymph sink.

Another variation is to incorporate trilobal nylon filaments of Antron into the fly to simulate the air bubble, much like the caddis in Gary Lafontaine's book, *Caddisflies,* Nick Lyons Books, 1981. LaFontaine's pioneering breakthroughs for imitating the plastron of emerging caddis are equally applicable to diving midges. Although not designed as such, his pattern for the Diving Caddis works just as well for swimming midges, and in trout waters as well as bluegill ponds.

Sometimes bluegill will smack the fly, but most often the fly is just sucked in; detecting the strike can be difficult. One approach is a greased-leader technique where silicone dry fly paste is applied to the leader, down to the beginning of the tippet. The 18 to 36 inch tippet is left bare so it will sink. You then watch the exact point where the leader breaks the surface tension of the water for the bluegill's subtle strike. At any twitch in the sunken junction briskly set the hook. The disadvantage to this method is that eventually the leader will start sinking, especially after you've caught a few fish.

Hand Twist Retrieve

Grasp the fly line between the thumb and first finger or first two fingers of your retrieve hand.
Pull an inch or two of fly line toward your palm. Rotate your wrist and recover more line with the other three fingers.

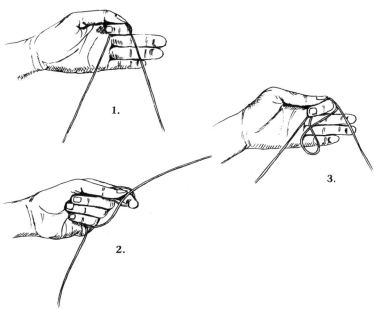

For many fish, the hand-twist retrieve is deadly, but if fishing is slow, before you change flies, vary your retrieve — make it slower or add a pause or two.

83

Another method is to use a strike indicator, the fly fisherman's bobber. The disadvantage of this method is that the bobber encumbers the casting stroke a bit with a light rod but it usually isn't that bad. You just slow your casting stroke a bit and widen the casting loop to compensate. Strike indicators include Cortland's adhesive-backed foam pads, a piece of brightly colored fly line without its core slipped over the leader ala Dave Whitlock, a siliconed, trimmed wad of fluorescent gift yarn tied onto the leader, or a steelhead drift fisherman's corkie, a tiny hollow plastic ball that has holes in each end to pass the monofilament through. A bushy dry fly will also work and will give you the chance to fish both surface and subsurface simultaneously.

The best retrieve is usually a slow one, or a slow retrieve interspersed with pauses. If your retrieve isn't working, before going to a faster retrieve, try slowing down. Bluegill prefer slow, sometimes just a mite faster than full stop. One of the most effective retrieves for bluegill is the hand-twist retrieve, partly because it is slow and partly because the fly line is always in your hand and you can readily set the hook.

The sunken fly will usually produce more fish and more big bluegill, but dry fly fishing for bluegill from a float tube is delightful.

DRY FLY BLUEGILL

Fishing a dry is the most effective when bluegill are rising or when they are holding within the top foot or so of the water column. Potshooting the rise is great fun — the idea is to lay out the fly so that it lands in the center of the bullseye where a bluegill has just risen. The fish is usually still close to the surface and under the rings of the rise. When the fly lands, the sensitive nerves in the fish's lateral line feel the vibrations and the bluegill will turn and take the dry.

Bluegill often feed in groups and if you miss the first fish, there is a second to attack the fly. If your fly doesn't immediately attract their attention, twitching the fly or slowly moving it a few inches will often do the trick. That's another

A float tube gives the angler tremendous freedom when fishing a lake; to the tuber the whole lake is readily accessible, no matter where the fish are feeding. Randy Gunn photo

advantage of using a light line rig — the lighter fly lines make very little disturbance when they land and don't spook the fish.

A stripped down Elk Hair Caddis is an excellent dry fly for bluegill. The Deer Hair Dry in size 16 is simply tied with a tightly dubbed dry fly type body and a cinched down deer hair wing. It floats well, sheds water with a crisp backcast, and has no hackle to impede hooking the fish.

When bluegill are rising to hatching midge pupae, a deadly fly is a trimmed Griffith's Gnat. The fly consists of a peacock herl body palmered with grizzly hackle. If you twist several herls with the tying thread to make the body the fly will last longer. The grizzly doesn't need to be high quality, but the hackle shouldn't extend out more than the hook gap in length. After the fly is tied, trim the hackle off on the top and bottom, leaving just the strands that stick straight out from the sides of the fly. This fly also has a high hook-up rate because the point of the hook is not masked by hackle.

You can dress the fly with silicone to help keep it afloat in the surface film, but the trimmed Griffith's Gnat is equally as effective just under the surface film. The Gnat should be left still, or merely twitched, or if it has gone subsurface, use a very slow hand twist retrieve to mimic the hatching midge.

I do all my bluegill fishing with barbless hooks because the hook point penetrates better, I catch more fish, and the fish are easier to unhook. That means more time for casting, hooking, and fighting fish, which is more fun than wrestling a barbed hook out of the small mouth of a bluegill.

BIG BLUEGILL

The little seven foot rod flexed pleasantly, sending the balanced fly line out in a smoothly unrolling loop, with the size 16 Deer Hair Dry just kissing the water as it landed as soft as a puff of cattail fluff. The twitch I gave the fly was squelched in a humping boil as a bull bluegill sucked in the tidbit.

The light rod bent into a deep horseshoe shape, its tip almost even with my eyes as the 'gill powered for the nearest cover in spurts of zigzagging energy. Just short of safety the bent spring of the fly rod forced the fish to the surface, to wind itself in helpless thrashing. The bluegill wasn't huge, but big enough to fill my hand and plenty of fish for the delicate fly rod.

Bluegill are the soldier ants of the piscatorial kingdom. They are highly efficient little beggars that police up any small prey organisms in their territory. They will feed on anything that moves and aren't intimidated by seemingly overlarge food items like wayward grasshoppers or waterlogged moths. Bluegill in turn are prey for bass and pike, but their evolutionary survival mechanism of reproduction to excess insures their survival. Their ability to adapt to almost any warmwater pond, their wholesale diet, and their fruitful egg-laying tendencies coupled with sexual maturity at 3 inches translates into fly fishing that is readily available all across the country.

Bluegill are valiant fighters, storming away from the fly rod in surging angled runs; they are belligerent fish that don't give up easily. But 90% of the countless bags of bluegill taken yearly consist of small fish.

By definition, a big bluegill is hand-sized, of more than 7 inches. A bluegill of that size will outfight most other 9 inch gamefish, including bass and trout. But finding these bigger bluegill requires specialized searching techniques and specific fishing strategies.

There are countless fishing spots all across the country where fish never see a fly because neither wading nor boating fishermen can get to them — but a float tuber can. Andy Anderson photo

Prime water for big bluegill must be rich in supportive aquatic life. There must be relatively stable banks, plenty of littoral (shoreline) vegetation for both cover and food-chain insects, ample deep-water spawning grounds for the bigger bluegill, and large enough bass or pike to limit the numbers of bluegill survivors.

Jumbo bluegill are the elite − they have successfully nourished themselves without being eaten. Ferretting out big 'gill water takes some investment in time and energy, both in finding a potentially good pond and in catching brawny bluegill.

There are two ponds close to my home that I regularly fish. They are both lovely little farm ponds; one produces the average-sized bluegill, the other has 7, 8, and 9 inch, and even an occasional 10 inch bluegill, a real heavyweight for northern waters (Oregon).

The pond with the bigger bluegill has more of everything. It is larger, has more vegetative cover, more aquatic insects (especially midges), more large bass, mostly deepwater spawning grounds where bass can prey on the young bluegill, and a vigorous population of hefty bluegill. Shoals of skittering baby bass vacuuming the littoral vegetation documents the hearty bass population, and even a 6 inch bass will prey on newborn bluegill. The lakelet is deficient in only one aspect − there are only a handful of fishermen that fish it.

The lack of fishing pressure as a contributing factor for healthy-sized bluegill goes against the basic bass/bluegill pond precept of save-the-bass, harvest the bluegill. Man as predator puts an artificial stress on fish populations, with certain predictable results. Given a free rein, we tend to overharvest, especially in our quest for the bigger (and biggest) fish.

If the goal is a dynamic population of jumbo bluegill, then the larger fish must be protected by the same catch-and-release philosophy that many fishermen and state agencies have adopted for bass and trout − releasing the best fish.

Harvesting small bluegill is undoubtedly beneficial for almost any pond, but the biggest bluegill should be released because they are the best survivors and most able to propagate the species. Just like bass and trout, the largest fish are the oldest, and it takes a winnowing of more than a few seasons to grow jumbo bluegill, especially in northern latitudes.

Big bluegill are the easiest to catch during the springtime spawning season and again in the fall when water temperatures drop and many bluegill spawn a second time. It's fun when the larger bedding bluegill slurp the traditional popper, but other strategies are needed to consistently catch the bigger 'gills all during the season.

The most precise presentation and potent pattern is useless if the fish are already spooked. Boat noise from motors, anchors, squeaky oarlocks, and oars or paddles splashing the water all scare fish — that's one of the biggest advantages of being a float tuber — you don't make any noise. Brian O'Keefe photo

Older bluegill exhibit some of the same movement patterns that bass use; the carousel of the seasons and the resultant weather and water temperature changes cause habitat preferences to change, too. The shallows will always hold some fish, but the beefy bluegill that successfully coexist with bass migrate in and out of the littoral feeding areas, usually in the morning and evening, along established routes like dropoff ledges and weedy points.

Weedbeds with a clear water ceiling of several feet are productive holding grounds for patriarchal bluegill. Although some big bluegill do spawn in shallow water, most covet the security of deepwater cover and go shoreward only far enough to feed around sunken vegetative reefs.

Temperature extremes of winter and full summer compress feeding time; December fish prefer an almost immobile tidbit in close proximity to their deepwater semi-hibernation grounds, whereas the August bluegill will migrate and vigorously feed, but only in the cooler hours of late evening and early morning. The fastest bluegill growth and the best fishing is in the spring, early summer, and fall months. Spawning stress consumes additional caloric energy, especially for fish that spawn in the fall, too. In the optimum water temperatures of the warm but not hot months, solid muscle tissue is added through day-long browsing in the aquatic larder.

The big bluegill fly rodder can borrow from the bass fisherman's repertoire of structure fishing strategies and systematic searching for the fish's preferred temperature level in the water column. The shallows are a logical starting place, especially in the spring and fall breeding periods.

One of the most productive areas for the fly fisherman in search of big bluegill is the first 20 feet out into the deeper water from the edge of the reeds, cattails, or lily pads. The larger 'gills like the ambience of more depth but proximity to vegetative aquatic insects and windfall terrestrials. A sunken weedbed or gradually sloping point interspersed with tendrils of vegetation can be a real hot spot for bull bluegill.

Water depth is crucial; the most potent fly pattern in the world won't produce jumbo bluegill if it isn't presented where the fish are feeding. When searching structure or probing for the preferred water column level with a fly, the most effective ploy for tangling with brawny bluegill is with wet flies that are compact but incorporate materials that move well, like rubber legs, marabou, or soft hackle.

At times bluegill will show a preference for a specific style of retrieve. The hand-twist is the best in most situations. A strip-and-pause or fast retrieve will occasionally excite a reluctant bluegill into striking the fly, but before trying that, be sure to slow the retrieve to a crawl. When they get finicky, bluegill, and especially big bluegill, most often show a rigid inclination to hit a slow fly, a fly manipulated somewhere between slowest and stop.

Sometimes jumbo bluegill will key into a particular type of structure. On one fall trip I discovered that the reeds held a particular attraction for the bigger bluegill that I was hunting. I cast to varied habitat like moss beds, sunken brush, and coves, but the only place that I nailed big bluegill was off reedy areas. It was a pattern the fish held for reasons of their own.

I remember one fish that was a late bloomer. My hand-twist nymph was barely plucked at about 5 feet out from the reeds about 3 feet underwater. I tightened, raised the rod, and felt resistance, but the fish swam towards me, apparently unalarmed.

Seemingly at the last minute, she saw me and powered for the bottom, almost bouncing the tip of the fly rod off my float tube fins.

The donnybrook was well fought; the light rod groaned down into the cork handle from her repeated steely plunges for freedom. I finally brought the 10 incher to hand, swollen with roe but in prime condition and a beautiful example of an elite bluegill.

NINE

LLAMA TREKKING

Cedar Lake squats at 6500 feet in Montana's Mission Mountains Wilderness Area, south of Kalispell in Flathead National Forest, about three miles in from the trailhead.

As I pull on my neoprene waders at the shore of Cedar Lake I can see an occasional dimpling trout. The riseform briefly mars the surface of the lake, cutting concentric rings in the mirror-top. In the September afternoon the eastern half of Cedar Lake's shore glows with a blaze of gold reflected in the changing leaves of Western Paper Birch trees and low slung thimbleberry and huckleberry bushes.

My muscles are tired from the hike, but finning out into the lake is easy work; the cool water soothes both body and soul. It's like floating in a giant aquarium, suspended in a soft gel that lulles me into tranquility.

No insects are hatching on Cedar Lake, but cutthroat are cruising here and there, looking for their evening meal. The surface film is littered with a sparse smattering of bugs: some caddis and Chironomid midges, aquatic and terrestrial moths and horse flies blown out into the water, beetles and wasps, and other assorted insects.

I position myself about 50 feet out from shore and make random casts, hoping to intercept a cruising cutthroat. The 3-weight graphite rod flexes slowly, landing 30 foot casts as delicately as a snowflake on sagebrush.

Since the food isn't concentrated in any particular spot, neither are the fish. The most consistent tactic is to cast a No. 10 Elk Hair Caddis to a likely spot, let it sit a moment or two, then twitch the fly a mite. If a trout doesn't take the fly after a few minutes I ease the fly in towards me a few feet, let it pause, then twitch it again.

That little twitch would sometimes grab a fish's attention; a cutthroat would take the dry in a quick splash. The light rod bent deep to the fish, even though they weren't big trout. Cedar Lake's slim bodied Yellowstone cutthroat average 10 to 14 inches.

While lounging in the float tube I detect a low humming sound emanating from the trees near our camp, the sound of contented llamas murmuring to each other.

Although our group had hiked in with daypacks loaded with cameras, binoculars, and snacks, the llamas did the real work of hauling our extra clothes, sleeping bags, tents, and cooking and fishing gear.

Trekking with a llama is like hiking with the family pet. Llamas not only look cute, they are gentle and wooley, with peaceful dispositions. They have big friendly eyes and noble banana-shaped ears that are distinctly llama.

The modern llama is a descendent of the guanaco of South America, although fossil evidence indicates that the original camelids roamed North America, spread to Asia and South America, then became extinct in North America about 10,000 years ago.

After Steve Rolfing hurt his back in a skiing accident in 1979, a friend suggested that Steve use a llama to transport his backpack.

That same year Steve and Sue Rolfing purchased Poncho, their first llama. Their second llama, Mistletoe, was

Although we had carried daypacks loaded with cameras, binoculars, and snacks, the llamas did the real work of hauling our extra clothes, sleeping bags, tents, and cooking and fishing gear, including waders, fins, and float tubes.

purchased in 1980 from Kim Novak and her veternarian husband, Bob Malloy. The Rolfings now have over 50 llamas on their ranch in Columbia Falls, Montana, just outside of Kalispell. But it is Poncho who has since earned the title of "most photographed" llama in the world, appearing on the NBC Today Show, and in magazines such as *Outside, Signature, Saudi Arabia Airlines, Honolulu Magazine,*

Sunset, Outdoor Life, and *Montana Magazine,* besides numerous national and regional newspapers including the Wall Street Journal and the New York Times.

Giggles and delighted yells echo across Cedar Lake as 5 1/2 year old Katie Rolfing and her dad catch cutthroat while fishing from a downed Douglas Fir; the half submerged tree provides an ideal fishing platform. Steve would cast out, hook a fish, then hand his fly rod to Katie. "Reel him in, Katie," Steve would say, chortling as Katie squealed in delight.

When sunlight no longer fell on the lake the trout stopped cruising, surface rises ceased, and Steve and Katie returned to camp.

Campside conversation drifts out to me as a blend of sporadic chuckling mixed with the clinking of kitchen tools. The hike and float tubing had honed my appetite to a keen edge so I paddle back to shore.

Under a canopy of Engleman Spruce and Douglas Fir, Steve putters here and there, melding an orchestra of pots and pans, cooking utensils and spices, creating a symphony of sweet smells on his Coleman stove.

Steve and assistant Mitch Hood serve a feast of orange and spinach lettuce salad followed by antelope strogonoff, and finished out with succulent home made apple cake.

I try not to gobble the tender bits of meat entwined with the noodles amid the rich creme sauce. The barbarian in me grunts with gastronomical pleasure as the light from the campfire reflects off this primal scene. The llamas give their blessing; a low hum passes from llama to llama — they are comfortable bedded down under the trees on this clear September night.

The other two members of the group are from McCall, Idaho: llama outfitter Cutler "Cut" Umbach; and retired District Forest Ranger for the Big Creek District of Payette National Forest, Earl Dodds.

We clear our palates with Stroh's beer and cool mountain water from the North Fork of Cedar Creek.

Steve says, "Llamas have been domesticated for 6,000 years, which makes them one of the first domesticated animals in the world. So they are highly efficient at what they do; they've been bred for packing and they do an excellent job."

Llamas are superb pack animals for several reasons. They can carry up to 100 pounds of gear even though the average llama only weighs between 200 and 250 pounds. They are calm and sure-footed on the trail, and like deer and elk, their feet have split toes and a padded heel, so wear on the trail is minimal. Even when fully loaded, llamas delicately pick their way on the trail at the same pace as their human hiker, perfectly quiet and perfectly under control. Llamas don't require packed-in hay; they browse on thimbleberry, fireweed, huckleberry, and various grasses.

Next morning the breakfast fare includes granola, eggs, and homemade cake, with juice or coffee.

Steve and Mitch load up the llamas, balancing each animal with side panniers for the three mile hike to Upper and Lower Ducharme Lakes. Steve straps his bright blue float tube on Moe, a llama known to us as the one "who will eat anything," being fond of what Mitch calls "people food" like carrots, apples, and peanuts.

Steve says, "Right now there are about 400 llamas in Montana and from 12,000 to 15,000 in the U.S. The demand for llamas far exceeds the supply. Part of the reason is that an import ban has been in effect since 1928 because of hoof-and-mouth disease in South America. So the only animals available are those raised in this country. A male llama is worth from $500.00 to $1,000.00. Gelded male llamas are used as the pack animals, and a trail-experienced llama is worth about $1500.00. Because of their breeding capability, a female llama is worth from $6,500.00 to $10,000.00."

Mitch says, "I read where a stud llama named "The Professor" sold at an auction in Los Angeles in March 1987, for $85,000.00."

The Aymara Indians of South America have a proverb that says, "To travel with llamas is to suffer."

But the modern hiker doesn't view hiking as a job that

means laboring over rough terrain and suffering from a lack of water, food, or other amenities. It is a joy to hike with llamas. It's like taking a step back in time with these ancient beasts of burden; llama trekking is more like pet trekking than herding onery beasts.

The trail switchbacks up through the timber as we gain altitude. Higher up we cross broken slabs of talus loosened by ancient glaciers that have gouged out a moraine valley. The llamas stride with a peculiar gait molded by their habit of walking with both feet of one side at the same time: left front and left rear, right front and right rear.

The llama I lead, named Charlie Brown, and the others, like Poncho and Moe, are trailwise veterans. Even a relative newcomer, Switchback, is calm and confident.

"They know right where to walk so they don't hang up their packs," Steve says.

High in the Mission Mountains Wilderness in Montana, Steve Rolfing of the Great Northern Llama Company casts to cruising West Slope cutthroat.

Float Tube Fly Fishing

At one point, some of the pack straps had loosened and needed adjusting. The llamas remained composed while Steve and Mitch retightened straps, yanked on buckles, and wrestled loads into place.

About halfway between Cedar Lake and Ducharme Lakes we stop for a rest at two unnamed lakes.

With these ancient beasts of burden, llama trekking is almost like taking a step back in time; but llamas are so calm that it's like hiking with the family pet.

"What do you call those lakes, Katie?" Steve says.

"I call one of them Deer Lake and the other one is Bunny Lake. I'm a good mountain girl," Katie says, while perched atop her special saddle on Poncho's back.

The last half mile of the hike to Ducharme Lake is cross-country bushwhacking, which illustrates what I call the "Inverse Trout Rule." That translates into the proposition that the farther you hike off the trail to a lake, the fewer people you will see, and quite often, the bigger the fish will be.

Upper and Lower Ducharme Lakes sit at 6,462 feet at the foot of the spine of the Mission Mountains Range, nestled in the vertebrae of the Rockies, amid granite crags pockmarked by fir and spruce.

Steve says, "Almost all these lakes have freshwater shrimp in them, which measure 3/8 to 5/8 inch. But for some reason the lakes with the big cutthroat have the West Slope cutthroat. The Yellowstone cutthroat don't seem to get as big. When the fish are biting, they will pretty much hit anything. Most of these lakes have bugs out during the months that I'm up here, so you're surface fishing with a floating line, which is the most fun."

Steve launches his float tube in Lower Ducharme Lake with Katie sitting on the bow of the float tube. Soon Steve is into a nice cutthroat, which Katie helps land.

Husky West Slope Cutthroat are willing in both Lower and Upper Ducharme Lakes – presently Cutler yells from his float tube in the upper lake, "Hey, I got a real nice one."

Cutler shows us his brilliantly marked 19-inch cutthroat that he fooled with a No. 10 Royal Coachman. Within minutes he backs that up with a 20-inch cutthroat that may go over three pounds.

"Boy, what a fish," he exclaims, removing the No. 12 Renegade from the trout's mouth.

Steve and Katie are catching cutthroat up to 17 inches, but I elect to join Cutler in Upper Ducharme, hoping for a bigger fish. I'm using an 8 1/2 foot 4-weight rod, which is light enough to enjoy the trout, but hefty enough to land a 20-inch fish.

Cutler and I catch some smaller trout, but the bigger fish

have turned off, so I go ashore and relaunch in Lower Ducharme. I've soon worn out a No. 14 Grizzly King and a No. 14 McGinty on nicely marked cutts to 17 inches, but none bigger. Still, it's a lovely afternoon spent "potshooting the rise," casting to cutthroat that are taking surface insects wherever they find them.

The evening campfire is more of the same – humming llamas, Steve reveling in contented puttering, and an excellent meal of Fettachini Alfredo with clam sauce, grilled and baked trout, grouse with apples and onions, marianated veggies with feta cheese, all capped off with homemade brownies.

That's the beauty of it – Steve, Mitch, and the llamas do all the work while you hike, fish, eat, and sit back and enjoy the wilderness. One of the joys of the high country in Montana in late September is the lack of mosquitoes. I saw nary a skeeter in our three day trip.

The last morning, breakfast is announced by a "Camp Robber," a Gray Jay looking to steal some camp scraps. This jay is also known as the "Canada Jay" and "Whiskey Jack." It stores scraps of food by gluing it into balls with its saliva and hiding the balls among the fir and pine needles.

Breakfast consists of eggs, granola, juice, coffee, and pancakes.

"Are these blueberry pancakes?" I ask Steve.

"No, they're huckleberry pancakes made from scratch with huckleberries we picked this summer. There's no romance in blueberry pancakes," he says.

When writer Tim Cahill of *Outside* magazine went on a trip with Steve in 1984, he complained that it seemed to him that llamas are without any negative characteristics. As an investigative reporter he had to reveal something "bad" about his subject – he couldn't say they were perfect. So Steve told him not to let a llama into your house. As Cahill wrote in the March 1985 issue, "Llamas are hell on houseplants."

Steve says, "At the risk of sounding corny, I feel there is something magical about llamas; there is something real special about being around them."

Steve and Sue Rolfing's Great Northern Llama Company runs llama trips from May through September, from day-hike picnics to several-day hikes along the Swan Divide of the Flathead National Forest. From the Swan Divide you can see Glacier National Park to the north, the Bob Marshall and Great Bear Wilderness Areas to the east, and the Mission Mountains Wilderness Area to the west.

Steve says, "We have several good trout lakes that we fish in the Swan Divide of the Flathead National Forest. We have our most openings in September, and we're often booked up for the summer by February."

For more information contact: Steve and Sue Rolfing, Great Northern Llama Company, 1795 Middle Road, Columbia Falls, MT 59912, (406) 755-9044, also: International Llama Association, P.O. Box 37505, Denver, CO 80237, (303) 699-9545.

TEN

FLIES

Flies for fishing from a float tube warrants a whole book in itself, a book on lake flies, particularly when covering a variety of species such as trout, largemouth bass, smallmouth bass, and bluegill.

Presented here is a basic selection of flies that will get you going and cover the majority of fishing problems you might encounter. But this certainly isn't the last word in lake flies, nor is it meant to be a complete listing.

TROUT FLIES

Most stream flies for trout will come in handy when fishing a lake, but there are some patterns you shouldn't be without when fishing a lake. Mainly because there are some organisms like leeches and crayfish that are prime fare in a lake that may or may not be present in any given stream.

Some good trout flies to include in your lake collection are the Adams, Compara dun, Mayfly Spinner, Elk Hair Caddis, Hare's Ear, and a Mayfly Emerger. The most common lake mayfly is the Callibaetis, and the spinner is just as important as the dun. Other trout lake flies include a Carpenter Ant imitation tied on a size 10 hook, a flying ant pattern in sizes 10 through 14, and a flying termite imitation, a Bucktail Caddis tied with a reddish orange body in size 10, 2xlong.

Griffith Gnat — excellent for midge hatches, particularly when the hackle is trimmed top and bottom. Imitates both the adult midge hatching out of its pupal shuck and the returning egg-laying females that get trapped in the surface film.

Griffith Gnat — George Griffith, founder of Trout Unlimited
Hook: Dry fly quality, standard length (Tiemco ring eye No. 101 hook is excellent for No. 18 and 20, two of the most often used sizes, followed by No.16.) sizes 10-20
Body: Peacock herl
Hackle: Grizzly palmered length of body

Damselfly nymph — damsels hatch in mid-summer, which means the nymph is available to fish until the emergence, when fish really key in on them. The nymph is slender and a slow swimmer, but an active predator on smaller nymphs. Damsels are bright green, olive, and tan.

Damsel Nymph — Polly Rosborough, winner of Buz Buscek Award
Hook: 2xlong or 3xl sizes 10 to 16
Tail: Marabou tufts to imitate sculling gills of nymph
Body: Yarn, dubbing, or twisted ostrich or marabou, slender, but build up thorax a bit
Wing: Marabou tufts

Dragonfly Nymph — there are many good imitations of the short rotund dragonfly nymph, which is usually olive brown. One of the most effective is the Carey Special, a simple pattern that simulates the swimming dragonfly. Randall Kaufmann's Floating Dragon is an excellent dragonfly nymph imitation, especially with a sinking or sinktip fly line.

Carey Special
Hook: 2xlong or 3xlong sizes 6 to 10
Tail: Pheasant tail fibers
Body: Peacock herl
Hackle: Pheasant tail fibers

Floating Dragon — Randall Kaufmann
Hook: 2xlong or 3xlong, sizes 4 to 10
Tail: Marabou tufts
Body: Spun deer hair
Legs: Marabou tufts
Wingcase: Dark mottled wing, such as dark turkey or peacock
Head Area: Yarn or dubbing
Eyes: Burnt monofilament, fairly large in diameter, or pre-formed

---

Any individual lake is like any individual stream; the physical and chemical makeup of each specific lake makes it unique and presents its own fishing problems.

Woolly Worm — a good imitation of the salt-and-pepper colored dragonfly nymph, but also a good generalist fly for many different types of lakes and varied species of fish besides trout, like smallmouth bass and bluegill. Some of the most effective combinations are grizzly hackle with black, brown, or olive body, or grizzly hackle that is dyed brown, brownish yellow, olive, or magenta.

Woolly Worm
Hook: 1x, 2x, or 3xlong, sizes 2 to 14
Body: Yarn, chenille, mohair, or dubbing
Hackle: Palmered, often grizzly

An effective Woolly Worm variation is the Woolly Bugger, which has a marabou tail added. The Woolly Bugger can imitate crayfish, leeches, or baitfish, depending on size and color of materials used.

Woolly Bugger
Same as above except add a tail of marabou and maybe a few strands of Crystal Flash or Flashabou.

Baby fish imitations often account for some of the biggest fish caught in lakes. The trick is for the angler to key in on the predominant prey available for big fish to attack. So one approach is to carry several types of streamers in various sizes and color schemes. Two of my favorite types are the Zonker and the Matuka.

Zonker — Dan Byford
Hook: 3xlong, sizes 2 to 10
Body: Silver, gold, or pearlescent mylar tubing
Wing: Rabbit fur strip, tied down front and back
Hackle: Grizzly or dyed saddle hackle

Matuka – originated in New Zealand by some sharp cookie
Hook: 3xlong, sizes 2 to 10
Body: Yarn, mohair, dubbing, or pearlescent tubing
Wing: Hen hackle, fat saddle hackle, or grouse
Rib: Copper, silver, or gold wire or tinsel
Hackle: Matched to wing material

Holding Water

In a day's fishing the float tuber might be presented with several different types of fish holding water. Point A is a shoal/shore area with the wind blowing surface food towards shore. Point B is a cliff with overhanging brush and deep water below. Trout will cruise this area looking for terrestrials. Point C is wood structure – in this case a log, providing shelter and habitat for food items. Point D is a combination of underwater and surface weeds. It is excellent habitat for all types of aquatic animals from shrimp (scuds) to dragonfly nymphs and small forage fish, plus provides safety. Point E is the boat dock which supplies large cover over relatively deep water which provides shelter and feeding opportunities for large fish. Fishing lakes is fishing structure.

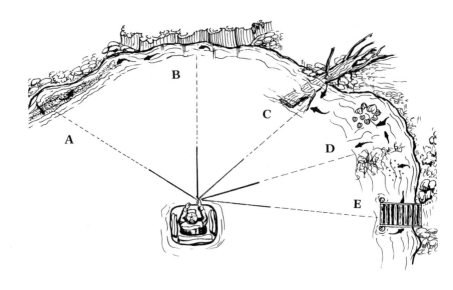

The freshwater leech is found in most lakes and is not overlooked by foraging trout. The aquatic leech resembles the common worm. It's body is long and slim and it swims like an undulating string. Since it's difficult to imitate a swimming string, leech patterns simulate life and movement by incorporating marabou, rough-dubbed fur, loose yarns like mohair, and soft webby hackle into the fly. Generalist flies like the Woolly Worm and the Woolly Bugger may also be taken by trout as leech imitations. Black, dark gray, olive, and dark maroon are good colors.

Marabou Leech
Hook: 2, 3, or 4xlong, sizes 4 to 10
Tail: Marabou
Body: Twisted marabou or fuzzy dubbing or yarn
Wing: Marabou

Fur Strip Leech
Hook: 2, 3, or 4xlong, sizes 4 to 10
Body: Fuzzy yarn or dubbing
Wing: Rabbit fur strip, tied front and back, or ribbed with fine wire
Hackle: Sparse grizzly to match body color

BLUEGILL FLIES

One of the most endearing facets of fishing for bluegill is their simplicity; a simple approach often works the best: trimmed down trout flies work very well. You can also use a miniature deer hair bass popper, but dry and wet trout flies work just fine. Picky bluegill feeding on midges can be duped with a Griffith Gnat.

Bluegill Soft Hackle
Hook: Standard length or 1xlong, sizes 14 and 16
Tail: Soft hackle such as grouse, partridge, hen chicken
Body: Fuzzy dubbing including guard hairs, in brown, black, and gray

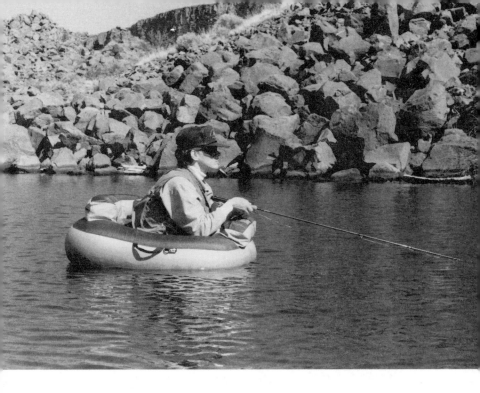

When using a full sinking line, you can better detect a light strike by keeping your rod tip underwater.

Rib: *Fine copper, gold, or silver wire*
Hackle: *Soft hackle similar to the tail material*

Bluegill Deer Hair Dry Fly

Hook: *Standard or 1xlong, regular wire or 1xfine, sizes 14 to 18*
Body: *Thin and tightly dubbed, in tan, yellow, or light brown*
Wing: *Deer hair cinched at the front ala Troth's Elk Hair Caddis*

LARGEMOUTH BASS FLIES

Predatory largemouth bass are most excited by big flies that incorporate lots of movement. A good strategy is to use flies that effectively exploit all the levels of the water column. Poppers for surface commotion, sliders for surface fishing with a more subtle presentation, Dahlberg Divers and neutral density flies for all levels, and flies like the Whitlock Eelworm Streamer or the Fur Strip Streamer for the bottom layers of the lake. Attractants like Flashabou and Crystal Flash added to the fly can excite a reluctant fish into striking.

Most Whit Hair Bug – Dave Whitlock
Hook: Tiemco 8089 or Mustad Stinger 37187, 1/0 to 10
Tail: Flared hackle tips and hackle collar, various color schemes
Body: Spun deer hair, various color schemes
Head: Trimmed spun deer hair
Eyes: Doll eyes with moveable black pupils
Snag Guard: Stiff .025 inch diameter monofilament (To promote surface disturbance, the popper is trimmed so that the face is flat. A slider is trimmed so that the head is more round and slides underwater with a minimum of disturbance for spooky bass feeding near the surface.)

Dahlberg Diver – Larry Dahlberg
Hook: Tiemco 8089 or Mustad Stinger 37187, 1/0 to 10
Tail: Flared dyed grizzly hackle tips, marabou, and Crystal Flash
Body: Spun deer hair with some flared to the rear
Head: A collar of trimmed hair is fanned out behind the head to plane the fly downward. The rest of the head is trimmed as a slider.
Snag Guard: Stiff .025 diameter monofilament (Besides being a good surface fly, the Dahlberg Diver is also effective when fished on a sinktip line with a short leader.)

Eelworm Streamer – Dave Whitlock
Hook: Tiemco 8089 or Mustad Stinger 37187, 1/0 to 10
Tail: Long soft dyed grizzly saddle hackle
Body: Lead wire on front half to sink fly and give it a jigging motion when retrieved. Yarn or mohair body.

Hackle: Palmered dyed grizzly
Head: Built up body material
Eyes: Bead chain eyes keep the hook riding up
Snag Guard: Stiff .025 diameter monofilament (Whitlock Eelworm Streamers are usually tied in black, blue, purple, yellow, and brown.)

SMALLMOUTH BASS FLIES

You should have a crayfish pattern for smallmouth and a simple pattern is often the most effective. Especially when you fish it right in among the rocks and underwater snags that are cover for fish. Other effective smallmouth flies include scaled-down largemouth poppers and snakey streamers like the Whitlock Eelworm Streamer and the Rabbit Fur Leech and also trout flies like leeches and baitfish imitators like the Zonker, Matuka, and Woolly Bugger. Besides the wide-gape bassin' Stinger hook, the Tiemco 8089 or Mustad 37187, you might investigate the Mustad forged Keel hook 79666, which is less snag prone because the hook point rides up in the water. Another option is to tie a snag guard.

Crayfish Fly
Hook: 3 or 4 xlong hook; or Tiemco 8089 or Mustad Stinger 37187, Mustad Keel, 79666, sizes 6 to 10
Tail: Tails imitate crayfish pincers; two pairs of flared-out dyed grizzly hackles in same colors as body. (Fly is tied backwards because crayfish swim backwards.)
Body: Lead wire is wrapped on the front half of the fly to help the fly sink and to give it a jigging motion on the retrieve. Chenille or yarn in crayfish colors of yellowish brown, olive brown, or maroon brown
Hackle: Palmered hackle up to head of fly, same color as body

ELEVEN

FLOAT TUBING TIPS

Modification is the middle name for many fly fishermen, which includes modifying float tubes and float tube paraphernalia. These tips may add to your float tubing pleasure.

FLOAT TUBE DEPTHFINDER
Plotting the bottom of a lake can give the angler valuable clues about dropoffs, ledges, sunken islands, and other fish attracting structure. One way to chart a lake bottom is with a simple plumb bob system. Attach a one ounce lead sinker to a line or cord and mark the cord with one stripe for every five feet, two stripes for every ten feet. Your depthfinder may be elementary, but it's small, lightweight, and most importantly, it works.

QUICK DEFLATION TOOL
By replacing the standard valve cap on a float tube with a valve core removal cap, you can keep dirt out of the valve

stem and use the tool to quickly deflate the float tube for compact storage. It's not a bad idea to have a spare valve core or two along, too.

FEATHERLIGHT PACKALONG ANCHOR

Even though a wind might come up, you can miss out on all that frantic finning by dropping anchor, a featherlight packalong anchor, and keep fishing. All you need is a nylon cord and a mesh bag that can hold a few rocks. If you don't have a mesh bag handy, you can use a square of nylon mesh or fiberglass window screen material that measures about two feet by two feet, or you can use the mesh bag used to pack onions at the grocery store.

Just fill your bag with rocks and tie it off with some of your anchor line. When you get to the fishing site, lower your anchor with the nylon cord. When you finish fishing, just unload the rocks. I keep the cord wrapped around a core of rolled up aluminum foil. The foil collapses nicely, doesn't weigh much, and I have some foil in case I need it.

A simple plumb bob makes an effective depth finder. As demonstrated, Randy Gunn used this method to locate the deep water dropoff in Oregon's Little Cultus Lake, which meant the difference between catching brook trout and getting skunked.

CARRY EVER-ESSENTIAL DUCT TAPE

The last time I fished Lake Billy Chinook for smallmouth bass I cut a small gash in the float tube cover on the sharp lava rocks by the launching site. To repair it, I let enough air out of the tube to expose the inside of the tear area. Then I put a strip of duct tape over the tear on the inner-tube-side of the float tube cover, filled the tube again, and went fishing. The tape is pushed tight against the float tube cover by the expanded inner tube and helps protect the inner tube.

Duct tape can temporarily repair broken fly box hinges, patch small leaks in waders (although Shoe Goo or Sportsman's Goop works better for neoprene waders), secure a rod guide to the rod until you get home, hold your reel securely to the rod if your reel seat loosens on your rod, and any number of small jobs.

A small roll of duct tape is always handy to have aboard. One way to store duct tape is to wrap it around a compact flashlight. You can wrap the first turns over some cord or monofilament so you can tie your flashlight to your vest, preventing the flashlight from falling into the water. You could tie a safety pin on the end for quick attachment to a D ring on your vest.

FLOATING FLY BOXES OR PLASTIC COATED UMBILICAL CORDS

The most sensible fly boxes for float tubing are those that will float if dropped into the water. Another way to safeguard your non-floating fly boxes is to attach them to your vest or float tube with a plastic coated umbilical cord. Use plastic coated steel leader material secured with crimpable sleeves; one end is permanently attached to the fly box while the other is crimped to a safety pin. Then, no matter where you stash your fly box, you can secure it to your vest, fishing shirt, or float tube pocket.

One float tuber I know keeps his forceps, hook hone, and other gadgets attached to his float tube via pin-on retractors. That way he already has all the tools he needs to

Using fly boxes that float makes perfect sense when float tubing.

fish, which eliminates the chance of either forgetting something important or losing an item overboard.

VELCRO ROD SAVERS

Many float tubes already have velcro rod holders attached to the casting apron of the float tube. When you need to change flies, unhook a fish, or change spools, you simply lift the velcro tab, slide your rod under the velcro, then press the velcro closed again. If your tube cover doesn't have velcro strips sewn on, it would be an excellent insurance policy to add them. In the excitement of changing flies or spools or unhooking a fish, it's just too easy to accidentally lose an expensive graphite rod and reel overboard. (I know of a father and son team who were fishing Crane Prairie Reservoir in central Oregon when the dad let his rod slip underwater – fortunately the son was able to snare one of the rod guides with his fly and save the outfit.)

DE-LIAR

If you are a catch-and-release fisherman who would like to know just how long that fish really is, but your tube lacks a stenciled-on tape measure, you can add one with a permanent magic marker. The front of the casting apron is usually the most convenient place to measure a fish, so that's where manufacturers place their stenciled-on ruler.

NETS AND CREELS

A net can be a handy item to have attached to your float tube for snaring those lunkers. Or at the opposite end of the spectrum, when you want to land (tube?) that 10-inch brook trout for dinner. Lifting a brookie out of the water by grabbing the tippet is a good way to set a trout free.

If you keep a fish, it also makes sense to have a stringer or creel with you. You can make a stringer from a length of cord or heavy monofilament about two feet long and two dowels about three inches long. The wood should be thick enough to not break but thin enough to go through a fish's mouth. Notch a ring around the center of the dowels so the cord or monofilament will have a groove to sink into when you tie on the dowels. The stringer is light, small, and can be kept in one of your float tube pouches until needed. It will float if dropped on the water and can be easily tied to a D ring on your tube when used.

The mesh bag idea that works for an anchor system also works as a creel, although you might want to rig up a drawstring closure for the top. That makes it easier to open the bag to put fish in and the drawstring closes tight to keep fish in the bag. Those inexpensive rubber lined creels that have been imported for years work well with a float tube because they are lightweight and not bulky.

PORTABLE COMPACT AIR COMPRESSORS

One of the handiest tools for the float tuber is the compact portable air compressor powered by a car or truck battery. Although a float tube inner tube isn't under a lot of pressure, at less than three pounds per square inch, there is a large volume of air in a 20 or 22 inch truck tire inner tube. You can pump up a float tube with a hand pump, but it takes a while. An automotive battery-powered compressor only takes about five minutes to inflate a float tube. These compressors are small and have an adapter that hooks into the cigarette lighter on the dashboard.

In my experience, a more expensive compressor doesn't necessarily pump any better than a less expensive model, and some of the top-line models aren't as reliable. You might be better off buying two cheaper compressors instead of one deluxe model, particularly if you are off in the boonies with nary a gas station in sight. I can assure you that it's a bitter ordeal to be looking out over an expanse of feeding fish when your deluxe compressor dies and your tube is only half filled with air.

After I burned up two deluxe compressors, I was told by the manufacturer that the reason the compressor failed was from a lack of back pressure from the float tube inner tube. In other words, it was explained to me that the compressor pump is designed to pump air against back pressure and if there isn't enough back pressure, the pump runs too fast and too hot and burns up. I don't understand the mechanical theory behind that, but that's what I was told. (The box the compressor came in stated that besides tires on cars, trucks, vans, motorcycles, mopeds, bicycles, garden tractors, riding mowers, and trailers, the compressor would inflate automotive air shocks, footballs, basketballs, soccer balls and all game balls, toys, balloons, RV water systems, air mattresses, and children's swimming pools.)

Apparently, float tubes don't fit into any of those descriptions. The same company came out with a "high output" air pump built with a fan as the pump instead of a compressor, designed for "large, low pressure inflatables," listing inflation times as 50 seconds for a 4-man boat, 20 seconds for a single air mattress, and 40 seconds for a sport tube.

So I spent 12 dollars on 24 inches of ¼ inside-diameter hose and fittings to modify the pump so it would attach to the float tube. But alas, the pump would only pump up the tube half way, then it just sat there humming away. I was told that because of the fan design, the pump wouldn't burn out. But it wouldn't pump up the float tube, either, in spite of the claim on the box of "extra volume for the big jobs."

Even when you use a fast retrieve, be sure to run the line between the fingers of your rod hand to maintain control of the fly line and to be able to detect the strike.

Float Tube Fly Fishing

It seems to me, considering that over 100,000 float tubes have been sold since 1980, some manufacturer could make a tidy profit marketing a reliable and effective portable compressor designed for float tubes.

As a precaution against either a leaking tube or a punctured tube I carry insurance. I'm referring to the aerosol cans of Fix-a-flat which inflate the tube and seal the leak at the same time with a latex sealant. With the inner tube protected by the heavy nylon cover it's unlikely you would ever sustain more than a small puncture. But it's those slow leaks that can drive you crazy. Fix-a-flat probably wouldn't completely inflate your tube but should stop small leaks and with the help of your portable air compressor or hand pump you would be right back out on the water. Although you would probably never need it, taking along a patch kit similar to a bicycle tire repair kit is also a good idea.

FLIPPER SAVERS

A nylon cord that is tied to your swim fin and then wrapped twice around your ankle and knotted will keep the fin from slipping off and being lost. It very seldom happens that a properly fitted fin will slide off your foot, but sometimes in the rush to go fishing, an angler won't get the fin strap securely fitted around the heel. A nylon safety line attached to your ankle insures that you won't lose your loose fin in some sticky lake bottom mud.

AVOID OVERINFLATION

One of the biggest dangers is overinflating the tube. Although you may start out with your tube at just the right pressure, it might change drastically. For example, suppose you launch in the early morning and then quit fishing by mid-morning. You place your tube under the shade of a tree and have lunch, then take a nap. The sun swings around, your float tube is in direct sunlight, the air in the tube heats up and expands. The same thing can happen if the tube is stashed in a truck canopy or van; as the interior of the van heats up, so does the float tube.

Another thing to watch out for is overexpansion due to a change in altitude. If you travel to a high mountain lake, be sure to allow for your tube expanding by as much as 20%.

Many float tube covers are designed so that the zipper will unzip if the tube is overinflated, so the seams won't burst. But not all tube covers are built that way.

Brian O'Keefe photo

More and more fishermen are going catch-and-release. Most fish populations can't hold up to the increased pressure of more and more fishermen, so most anglers are limiting their kill and turning loose the bigger fish. It makes particularly good sense to turn loose the big fish because those are the choice spawning fish and by killing them you may be harming your fishery. Why not have the thrill of catching that big hog over and over again instead of just once?

Aquatic Plants

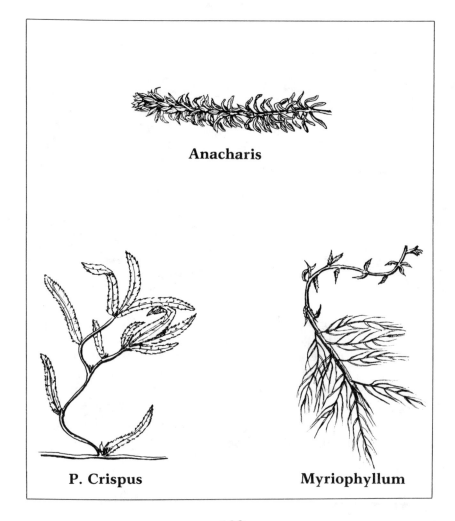

Anacharis

P. Crispus

Myriophyllum

Nuphar

Lily Pads

Valliseria

Index

122